SOCIAL SECURITY FINANCING

International Labour Office - Geneva

First published 1997

ISBN 92-2-110736-1

Author unit: SEC/PDN
Editor: T. Whitaker
Designer: P. Bissaca, E. Fortarezza
Production: International Training Centre of the ILO, Turin, Italy

PREFACE

This manual is one of a series produced by the Social Security Department of the International Labour Office, Geneva. It was prepared in conjunction with the International Training Centre of the ILO, Turin, and the International Social Security Association, Geneva.

Other publications in the series:

- Social Security Principles
- Administration of Social Security
- Pension Schemes
- Social Health Insurance
- A Trainers' Guide

The manuals have been produced primarily for use in countries where social security systems are not yet operational, are undergoing change or need to be improved. In particular, the manuals will be useful in developing countries, countries in transition, and countries undergoing structural change, as they begin the process of setting up new systems of social protection or of improving existing systems.

It should be noted, however, that the information contained in the manuals refers almost entirely to the formal sector and not to the wide range of systems which apply to groups outside the traditional social security system.

It will be apparent that, in a manual of this size, it is possible to provide only a broad overview of the topic. For the reader needing more extensive or detailed information about Social Security financing, there may well be a need for additional reading. There is a wide range of publications which deal with the topic in greater depth and some of these are referred to in the additional reading list at the end of this manual.

Thanks are due to all those people - too numerous to mention individually - who have helped in the preparation of this manual. In particular, the assistance of the International Social Security Association (ISSA) is acknowledged.

Should any reader wish to provide comments or feedback on the contents of this or any other manual in the series, please write to:

The International Labour Office,
SEC/SOC, 9th Floor,
4 route des Morillons,
CH-1211 GENEVE 22,
Switzerland.
Fax (22) 799.7962

TABLE OF CONTENTS

SOCIAL SECURITY FINANCING

MODULE 1:
SOCIAL PROTECTION SYSTEMS
AND
THEIR ECONOMIC ENVIRONMENT

International Labour Office - Geneva

MODULE CONTENTS

UNIT I: **Macro-economic dimension and social impact**

     A.   Social protection systems: Components and functions

     B.   The macro-economic dimension of social protection

     C.   The inter-relationship between social protection and the national economy

UNIT 2:   **Specific economic issues**

     A.   General economic considerations

     B.   Income redistribution

     C.   Incidence of contributions

     D.   Labour market: Employment and production

     E.   Consumption and demand

     F.   Savings, capital formation and investment

MODULE 1

SOCIAL PROTECTION SYSTEMS AND THEIR ECONOMIC ENVIRONMENT

UNIT I: Macro-economic dimension and social impact

A. Social protection systems: Components and functions

National social protection systems are not economic islands. Depending on the level of development, national social protection systems redistribute between 10 and 30 percent of the gross domestic product (GDP). They thus embody one of the major redistributive mechanisms of national economies. Before the financing techniques for individual sub-components of national social protection systems are discussed, a basic notion of the interactions between the economy as a whole and the redistributive mechanisms of social protection is required to understand and accept the macroeconomic constraints within which each national social protection system is operating.

Components

Formal social protection systems may be conceived in terms of four components:

- social security systems – statutory employment-related benefits (pensions, short-term cash benefits, social health insurance);

- universal social benefit systems – benefits for all residents (family allowances, public health services, demogrants for old age);

- social assistance systems – poverty alleviation benefits, in cash and kind, for citizens and residents in special need;

- private benefit systems – employment-related or individual benefits (occupational pensions, employer-provided health insurance).

When governments mandate public social protection systems, commanding the redistribution of a substantial part of the society's income, they are obliged to ascertain that the systems are well managed and that resources entrusted to them are spent carefully and responsibly. Key staff of all social protection subsystems have to be well trained in management techniques as well as techniques for financial management. The techniques used to finance social security schemes which, in quantitative terms, are the dominant subsystems of most national social protection systems, can in large part also be applied to the other components of national social protection systems.

Functions

Modern social protection systems have two basic functions:

- **a safety net** function, which should ensure that each member of society who is facing destitution is provided with the minimum level of cash income, health and social services which allow the member to lead a socially meaningful life;

- an **income maintenance** function, which permits economically active members of society, or all residents, to build up entitlements which allow them to maintain a decent standard of living during periods of unemployment, sickness, maternity, old age, invalidity and survivorship, when other forms of income and activity are not possible.

Social protection systems need not be confined to reacting to situations created by economic and political changes. They can facilitate economic transition or development by providing a benefit delivery system that promotes economic development (which can include restructuring of the economy and the labour force). The key problem, for social protection policy makers in any economy, is to find an appropriate combination of the alleviation and prevention functions of the social protection system and, at the same time, actively support the process of economic development or change.

It is recognized that social and economic development must proceed together, and that careful design of social protection programmes, and judicious allocation of resources to them, can further the objectives of both social and economic development. Social security is one of these social programmes. In any country there is a level of social security which is appropriate to its administrative infrastructure and capacity, and the stage of economic development which has been reached.

The identification and detailed formulation of this level, so that the greatest degree of social protection is afforded for the resources that are allocated to social security, is a major challenge facing national planners. In countries without existing social security programmes, planners can endeavour to design the optimum programme. Where schemes already exist, the process is more difficult because planners will inevitably be confronted with institutional rigidities and reluctance to change. Nevertheless, the scarcity of resources, and the need to ensure that they are utilized to the best advantage, mean that planners must continue to improve the level and efficiency of social security protection.

Alternative economic strategies can be evaluated using quantitative analysis to assess their potential impacts and achievements. The social impact and economic effects of resources devoted to social security programmes – programmes which produce, for example, a healthier population or lead to increased productivity, or which reduce poverty – are often overlooked or underestimated, because they are sometimes difficult to measure or because analysts are not familiar with the techniques that allow quantification of their effects. Nonetheless, a balanced assessment of the economic effects of implementing new social security measures cannot confine itself to analysis of the short-term impact of social security contributions, or the fiscal and financial implications of the scheme. They must also take into account the potential long-term effects of the social security programme on the behaviour of the labour market and society in general. The complex interactions of many factors, and the long-term nature of many of the effects, mean that any assessment of their economic impact must be made over an appropriately long time frame. Economic estimates which are of limited dimensions, and which are made without taking these elements into account, can be misleading and do not contribute to a balanced assessment of the economic viability and impact of social security programmes.

The concept of trade-offs is central in economics. Any increase in social security expenditures means that all other expenditures, as a group, must decrease. If the government has a fixed budget, increases in social security expenditures reduce other government expenditures. For example, increases in social security expenditures to provide old-age pensions may cause reductions in medical expenditures for the old age group. While increasing social security expenditures may be desirable, those expenditures must be balanced against other worthwhile expenditures. It is difficult to pinpoint what is being sacrificed when social security expenditures are increased and, in reality, the sacrifice may be a slight reduction in a number of expenditures. Nevertheless, in policy analysis it is useful to question whether an alternate expenditure would benefit more the elderly or society generally.

In most countries, basic structural changes are occurring, many of them triggered by national policies, development plans, and market forces. In developing countries, this includes the shift from rural subsistence employment to urban money wage employment and, as a consequence, family support systems are becoming less dependable. In order to meet the needs of workers and their families who are participating in these adjustments, social protection – different from the rural social protection through plots of land or the help of the extended family or village community – must be provided. Some employers are willing and able to provide part of this protection to their workers, and this voluntary provision of employee benefits should be encouraged. Nevertheless, for most workers in the formal sector in developing countries, the prinicipal social protection will be that which is mandated by the government.

B. The macro-economic dimension of social protection

The following charts (Figures 1 and 2) present the relationship between the level of overall public spending on social protection and the level of GDP per capita in selected countries, at different levels of economic development. This has two major aspects:

(1) as can be seen from the difference in social spending, between developing and industrialized countries, there is a positive relationship between the dimension of social spending and the level of per capita GDP; but

(2) between countries on a similar level of GDP per capita, there are considerable differences in the level of public social spending.

The explanation for the two phenomena comes in two parts. The share of GDP that countries can allocate through the social protection systems is clearly limited by

(a) the share and level of directly taxable formal sector income in GDP, the amounts of other macro-economic aggregates (for example consumption, imports and exports) that can be taxed, the administrative and logistical capacity to cover a wide proportion of the total population by formal social protection systems, and the accessibility of the population to such systems;

(b) societal values and political priorities in each country with respect to the distribution and the use of total national income.

One of the key questions that national planners have to answer is: How much do we want to spend on social protection?
In view of the social needs, in particular in developing countries, the question is generally transformed into: How much can we *afford* to spend on social protection?

**Figure 1: Public social protection expenditure as a
percentage of GDP**

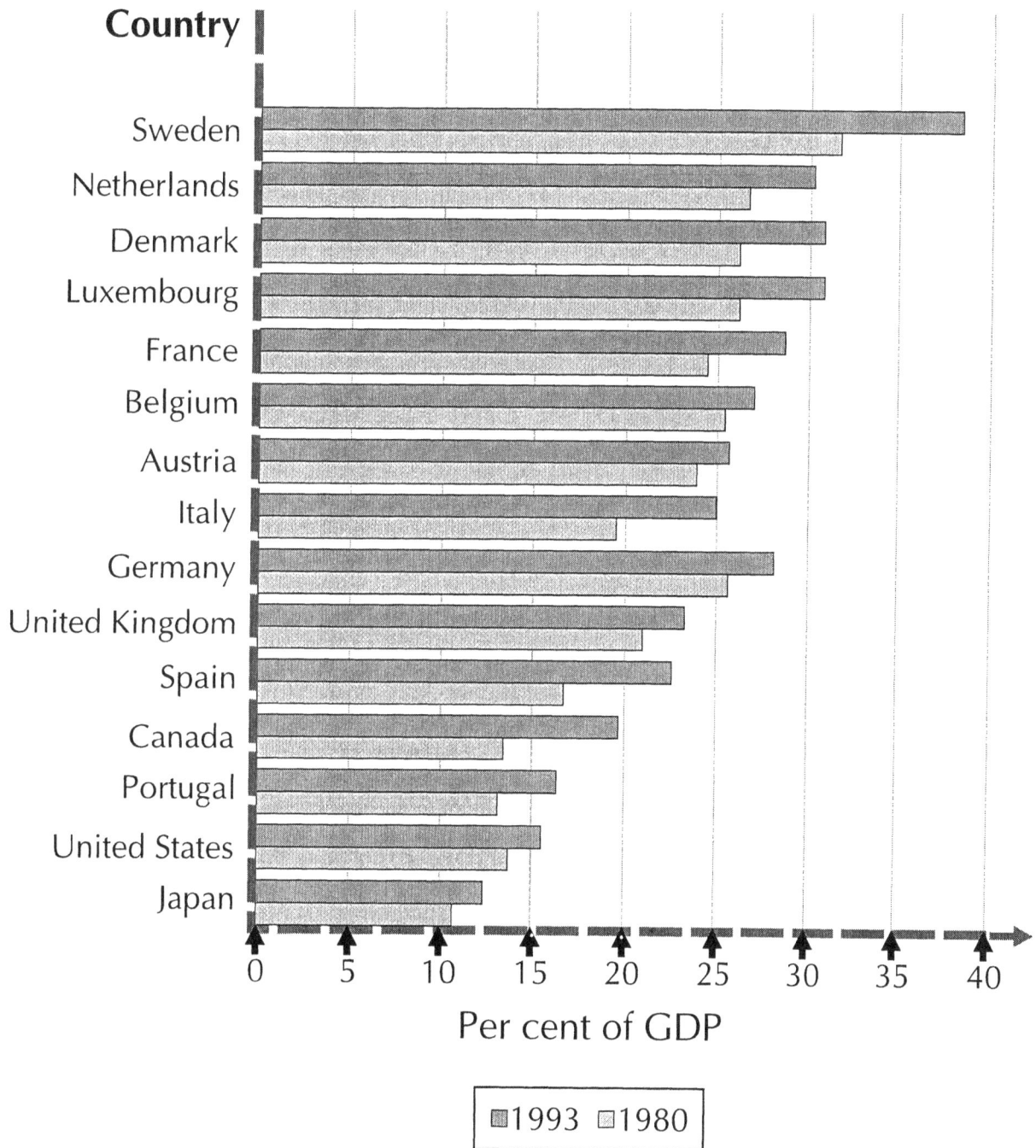

Per cent of GDP

■1993 □1980

*Source: OECD, **SOCIAL EXPENDITURE STATISTICS OF OECD MEMBERS COUNTRIES,**
LABOUR MARKET AND SOCIAL POLICY OCCASIONAL PAPERS, No. 17, Paris, 1996.*

**Figure 2:   Social security benefit expenditure as a
percentage of GDP**

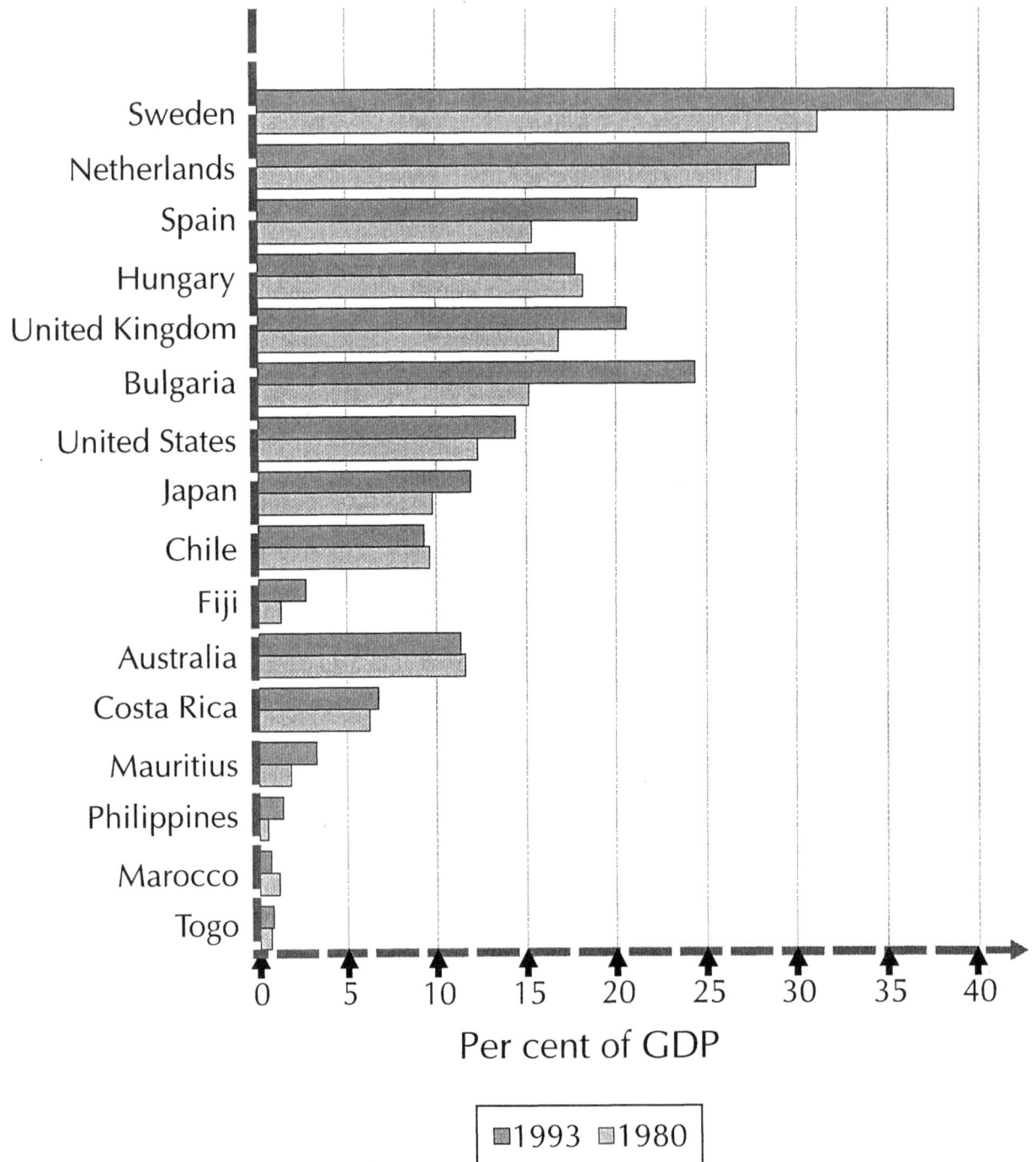

Per cent of GDP

■1993 ▣1980

For Mauritius data available reflects 1981 and 1990 values.

*Source: ILO's Inquiries into the **Cost of social security**, Geneva, various years.*

It is intuitively clear that a Western European level of social protection cannot be financed out of the GDP of a developing country. However, the priorities of each society play such an important role in determining the level of social protection that there can be no universal rule about what is economically affordable.

A significant part of social expenditure is usually financed by employees through social security contributions and earmarked taxes, either directly through contributions and taxes paid by employees or indirectly through foregone wages (employer contributions being thought, by most economists, to be borne by employees in the form of lower wages). Constraints on social expenditure are generally revenue constraints rather than expenditure constraints. One of the main revenue constraints is social. In any society there are limits to solidarity. This limit is reached when employees, or taxpayers in general, will not accept the financing of further public expenditure through deductions from their income as social security contributions and direct and indirect taxes. The overall limit might be higher if a major share of the total financial burden of the social protection system is derived from social insurance contributions where usually a personal link between contributions and benefit entitlements is established and where contributors perceive a personal gain from contributions. The limit can be identified only very inaccurately by behavioural signals sent out by the populace, in the form of open political resistance to a further increase of the "fiscal load" or increased evasion.

In summary, the key constraint under which social security planners are operating is the fact that resources for social security – as for virtually all other resources in an economy – are scarce. The financing techniques, used in the management of social security, should make the most efficient use of available resources.

C. The inter-relationship between social protection and the national economy

The following diagram illustrates the most important inter-relationships between the economy as a whole and the social protection system – a major financial and economic subsystem.

Figure 3: The inter-relationships between the social protection system and the economy

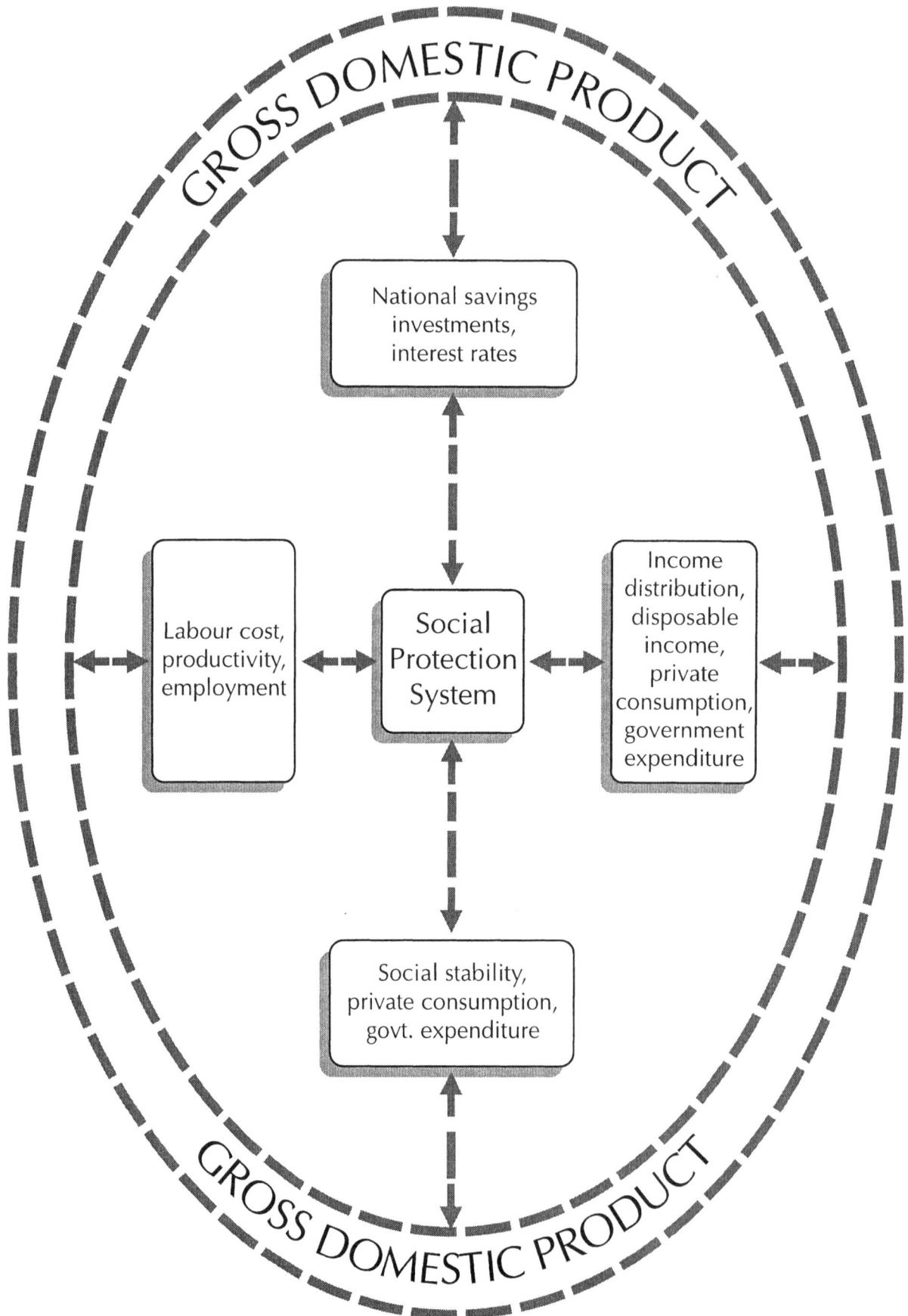

GROSS DOMESTIC PRODUCT

National savings
investments,
interest rates

Labour cost,
productivity,
employment

Social
Protection
System

Income
distribution,
disposable
income,
private
consumption,
government
expenditure

Social stability,
private consumption,
govt. expenditure

GROSS DOMESTIC PRODUCT

The social protection system influences income distribution directly by the redistribution of resources, which are collected through contributions or taxes from certain economically active individuals, enterprises and institutions, to certain other dependent individuals. Thus, it influences the distribution of income and consumption between different households and hence, indirectly, may also alter their total. This impacts on the structure and volume of aggregate demand, and thus on GDP.

Social security financing generally implies costs for employers which might (if wages are not flexible downward) add to their labour cost. There is a wide debate on whether social security charges (contributions or payroll taxes) are, de facto, borne by employers or not. If the supply of labour exceeds the demand, it might well be that all surcharges are actually just reducing the wages of workers, and the cost of social security schemes is thus in fact borne by workers. But still these social security charges might reduce formal sector employment on the fringes of the labour market, notably of low-paid workers in small enterprises. If wage levels are not flexible, high social security contributions or taxes increase labour costs borne by employers, and hence might have a broader negative effect on employment. On the other hand, social security measures (for example, health insurance, sickness benefits, health and safety measures related to employment injury insurance, rehabilitation and unemployment benefits which give workers time to find the right job) might increase the productivity of workers and thereby reduce the unit labour cost. The net overall effect on labour cost, productivity, and employment, is determined by the specific conditions in each national economy or even in each economic sub-sector. In any case, social protection measures will influence GDP through the labour cost-employment-productivity connection.

Social protection measures help to create or maintain social stability. Social stability stimulates the domestic demand for goods and services, which in turn drives GDP.

Social protection measures also affect the level of national savings and investment. If workers are provided with reliable social security provisions they might be inclined to save less or more; the quantitative evidence for this relationship is not very strong. Social protection systems which accumulate reserves may also influence total national savings. National savings as well as the pattern of savings (individual vs. institutional) influence the structure and volume of national investment and investment, in turn, impacts on GDP.

Gross national product itself, as well as the distribution of income in the economy, in turn influences the volume of resources that can be allocated to social protection.

The following sections discuss the specific aspects of this web of inter-relations in more detail. Before the economic aspects are scrutinized it is useful to briefly state the intended social effects of social protection systems.

Social effects

What are the main social effects generally attributed to implementing appropriately designed social security measures?

- The provision of medical care (including preventive measures) will improve the health of workers and their families. Safety and health at the workplace can be improved by allocating resources from an employment injury scheme to occupational safety and health programmes.

- Provision of a retirement pension means that a worker no longer needs to rely on family support.

- Income replacement schemes result in workers and their families having greater economic and psychological security, and hence greater stability. Through horizontal redistribution, income replacement can allow consumption and thereby living standards, to be maintained in times of adversity and, especially, unemployment.

- Provision of portable retirement benefits will make private sector employment more attractive, and mobility of labour will be encouraged.

- Provision of a retirement pension will encourage workers to leave the active labour force when they become eligible for the pension, thereby creating openings for new entrants.

- Vertical redistribution can be introduced through progressive contribution structures and targeted benefits, thereby reducing income disparities.

- By introducing and extending social security measures government gives a signal that it is cognizant of the needs and the importance of workers and their families, and that it does not regard labour only as a means to achieve economic growth.

The extent to which these social effects interact and apply in the long term depends on the nature of the society and the provisions of the social security programme. While improved health, stability and motivation of the labour force will result in greater productivity and contribute to economic growth, the timing and extent of this contribution is not possible to quantify.

UNIT 2: Specific economic issues

A. General economic considerations

An important consideration in the economic analysis of a new or expanded social security programme is the pace at which it will be introduced. Employers and investors do not react favourably to surprises, and narrow economic analysis of a scheme which provides for substantially expanded coverage and/or higher contribution rates will inevitably lead to dire prognoses if it is assumed that the expansion will take effect immediately. In developing countries, expansion of coverage and more energetic enforcement of participation can only be accomplished gradually. Hence, economic analysis focusing on the effect of expansion of a programme or a higher contribution rate can be misleading unless it takes into account that, normally, these measures must be implemented over several years.

A social security programme must be financially sustainable and economically non-distortionary. While the government provides an explicit or implicit guarantee of social security benefits, in a developing country where the compulsory state social security scheme protects only a small portion of the labour force, the programme should be financed so that it will not require a subsidy either directly or indirectly from the government budget. Such subsidies, from general taxation to a benefit programme for a minority, would not be equitable. The need for subsidization by public funds can be avoided through proper design of the benefits and the application of appropriate financial systems.

B. Income redistribution

Social security programmes which follow insurance principles, or offer a benefit in kind (such as medical care) help people to smooth their incomes and to maintain their standard of living when not earning or when sick. A social insurance scheme, with periodic payments provides income security which, in countries where there are great disparities in wealth, can contribute to the reduction of social tensions. This is achieved through the income redistribution effects of a social insurance scheme. The extent to which a scheme is redistributive depends on the design of the benefits and the source of the contributions (workers, employers and government).

A social insurance scheme can redistribute income "horizontally" among workers covered by the scheme who are (or were) in the same income groups; for example, from active workers to retired workers, or from active workers to those who are on sick leave. "Vertical" income redistribution means the shifting of income from those with higher incomes to those with lower incomes. This can occur, for example, in a social insurance pension scheme where lower-paid workers receive pensions based on a higher percentage of their earnings than do higher-paid workers, and where the contributions of all workers are the same percentage of their pay. Similarly, in a scheme which provides medical care, or other benefits in kind, and where contributions are a fixed percentage of earnings, vertical redistribution often occurs. A social insurance scheme providing cash benefits can be designed to achieve whatever level of vertical income redistribution is desired. Because they are individual savings schemes, defined-contribution schemes (e.g., provident funds) do not result in any vertical or horizontal income redistribution.

A social insurance scheme can also redistribute income from the working phase of life to the retirement phase. Economists view most people as making decisions by taking into account effects of their current actions on their future income. When viewed only in the context of the current period, contributions to a defined benefit social security scheme are a tax on workers that is used to finance transfers to retirees. However, when viewed in a lifetime context, people realize that contributions increase their future social security benefits. The exact relationship between contributions and benefits is determined by the benefit formula. In periods when contributions do not increase benefits, the single period perspective applies and social security is a tax. In periods when there is a connection between contributions and benefits, if the present value of the future benefits accrued equals the contribution, the tax is exactly offset by future benefits. Then from a life cycle perspective contributions are mandatory savings.

A social insurance programme may produce income redistribution from urban to rural areas, among occupations, or among regions of a country. This redistribution does not usually result from the design of the social security scheme, but depends rather on the extent to which participants take up benefits (e.g. medical care, cash benefits for sickness or maternity), whether they retire to rural areas, and other factors independent of the scheme itself.

Any income redistribution can benefit only those persons who are covered by the social insurance scheme. In developing countries, coverage typically extends only to persons in wage and salaried employment, and schemes are often criticized for this restriction because, in most of these countries, the vast majority of workers are rural agricultural workers who also need the protection afforded by social security. This is obviously true, but the coverage of these workers, many of whom may not be in the cash economy, presents formidable problems regarding the design of appropriate benefits and the administration of the scheme.

On the other hand, workers in wage and salaried employment are normally found in urban areas, to which they and their dependants have migrated leaving behind their extended families and the community support which this implies. While these workers may already be favoured, by virtue of living in an urban area and having access to wage and salaried employment, they nevertheless need social security protection because they cannot rely on support from their extended families. Also, these workers contribute directly to the industrial development of the country, and the provision of social security to them furthers that development. It would be inequitable for a government to allocate general tax revenues to finance a social security scheme restricted to urban workers only and, in developing countries, these schemes are normally financed entirely by contributions from the workers and their employers, without any current or anticipated state subsidy.

C. *Incidence of contributions*

While the payment of social security contributions is set in the legislation, a question which often arises is: Who actually bears the cost of the contributions? Are employers' contributions deferred wages of workers? Do employers pass the burden of their contributions on to consumers, in the form of higher prices, or do they hold down workers' wages (or wage increases) to recover the amount of their contributions? As stated above, most economists favour the latter hypothesis. Do workers demand wage increases to compensate for the contributions they are required to pay? Clearly, there are limits to these alternatives, but even if workers' wages were held down, provided the contributions produced meaningful benefits which adequately protected workers and their dependants, any wages which were foregone would tend to be balanced by the protection afforded.

The burden of financing public expenditure on social programmes is difficult to discern. The participation of the public authorities is very often financed through the ordinary State budget, where the revenue is produced through direct and indirect taxes and fees. Consequently, it is impossible to say whether the part allocated to social security comes from one or another income item in the State budget. Even if it were possible to assess the short-term effect of such taxes, as in the case of special taxes earmarked for social security, it would be extremely difficult to determine the final incidence.

In principle, contributions or payroll taxes that are proportional differ in their impact from income taxes, which in principle are generally progressive. However, many countries have introduced floors and ceilings on insurable earnings that alter the proportionality and the degree of progressivity or regressivity. It is necessary, however, to consider not only the social security contribution rate but also the benefit structure, and particularly whether there is an element of redistribution of income from higher- to lower-paid workers in the benefit provisions.

As the decision on the sources of financing has to be made on the basis of the particular conditions prevailing in the individual countries, ILO standards do not make any detailed provisions in this respect and leave the matter of financing to be largely dealt with by the national legislation. The Social Security (Minimum Standards) Convention, 1952 (No.102) provides that the cost of the benefits and administration shall be borne collectively, by way of insurance contributions or taxation or both, in a manner which avoids hardship to persons of small means and which takes into account the economic situation of the member country and of the classes of persons protected. The Convention provides, furthermore, that the total insurance contributions, borne by the employees protected, shall not exceed 50 per cent of the total of the financial resources allocated to the protection of employees and their wives and children. The Convention also requires that the member State shall accept general responsibility for the due provision of the benefits provided in accordance with the Convention; however, this does not mean that the State is obliged to participate in a regular way in the financing of the scheme.

D. Labour market: Employment and production

There are two extreme viewpoints concerning the effect of social security on production and employment. On the one hand, benefits are generally spent to meet current needs, therefore they sustain a higher level of demand for goods and services which, in turn, leads to a higher level of employment than would otherwise be possible. On the other hand, it is argued that the cost of providing benefits is a significant economic burden.

If social security is financed exclusively by contributions from workers and employers (as is the case in nearly all developing countries) two observations are sometimes made. Workers may claim that contributions place an unfair burden on low-income earners, and may create or worsen poverty among them. In the case of employers, there are two related arguments. First, it may be claimed that, in domestic markets, social security contributions raise production costs and reduce profitability, thus encouraging employers to seek more capital-intensive methods which inevitably lead to reduced levels of employment. Second, concerning international markets, employers may argue that, by increasing production costs, the contributions make their products less competitive with those of producers in countries where social security contributions are lower or even non-existent, leading to reduced exports.

In considering these arguments, it should be noted that high employers' contributions may well lead to lower cash wages, so that total labour costs would not be affected. It may also be noted that, among countries competing in international markets, there is no clear evidence that those countries with low social security contribution rates have achieved significant gains over those with high rates. (An example of this is the European Union, where the employers' contribution rates vary considerably.)

Ultimately competitiveness is affected by productivity, of which labour productivity is only a part. The way this is perceived by trading partners is also influenced by exchange rates. Moreover, social security contributions are generally only a small part of total labour costs; much more important are wages, and there are other costs associated with provisions for safety and welfare of workers. Since the employer's contribution is allowed as a business expense, the State is providing a subsidy to the social security scheme in the form of taxes foregone. If social security costs are relatively unimportant, attempts to manipulate the sources of contributions to social security are unlikely to have a significant effect on production and employment.

Workers and employers may seek to shift the economic incidence of social security contributions on to each other, the former by seeking compensatory wage increases and the latter by deferring future wage increases. Employers may seek to shift the cost on to consumers, thereby increasing the cost of living and reducing international competitiveness of export industries. Alternatively, employers may maintain prices and absorb the additional cost by increasing output. As productivity improves this alternative becomes increasingly possible. If the contribution burden on employers is considered excessive, efforts can be made to substitute capital for labour. The ultimate effect on the demand for labour and economic growth will be a complex combination of all of these factors depending on the marketplace, the labour market, the capital cost of changing production methods, improvements in the productivity of labour and the strength of workers' organizations.

Social security may affect the job or sector of employment a worker chooses when workers seek to avoid making mandatory contributions. Evasion and contribution avoidance are closely related concepts. Evasion is not paying contributions that are legally required for a particular job. Avoidance is choosing a job where contributions are not legally required. Evasion may involve choosing a job where the worker can evade paying social security contributions even though legally required to do so. Thus, both evasion and avoidance may affect a worker's choice of job. An important factor affecting evasion and avoidance is whether the worker views the mandatory contributions as a tax.

Social security can play an important role in the generation of employment if reserve funds accumulated by the scheme are invested in productive enterprises. The capital generated by social security schemes can constitute a significant proportion of domestic capital formation. Even if the social security funds are allocated to government securities, this allocation reduces the government's demand for funds from other sources, and frees them for investment in enterprises.

Social security can also affect employment in the labour market by affecting the age at which workers retire. Both defined benefit, and defined contribution, social security schemes may affect a worker's decision to retire, by providing an old-age pension when otherwise the worker would not have adequate retirement savings to retire. Social security may also affect retirement in other ways. In many defined benefit social security schemes, workers may not receive a pension and continue to work, unless their earnings are below a certain level. This earnings test may cause some workers to retire in order to receive benefits. However, pensions may sometimes be increased by postponing the age of first receipt of benefits. If workers were myopic, they would not take into account the increase in future benefits in deciding when to retire. Using a lifetime perspective, workers will take into account the increase in future benefits that occurs with postponed retirement, which will encourage them to retire later than otherwise.

E. Consumption and demand

Workers' contributions to social security constitute a reduction in their disposable incomes, and the periodic benefits which are paid replace at least a portion of these incomes. A reduction in consumable income implies a lower level of discretionary expenditure and, in particular, lower demand for luxury and semi-luxury goods. This reduced demand can also have the effect of mitigating inflation and, in some countries, an increase in the social security contribution rate has been used to achieve this objective.

The income replacement provided by periodic cash benefit payments permits workers and their dependants to sustain themselves during the contingency (e.g. sickness, retirement) which gave rise to the benefit. In other words, the periodic payments permit them to maintain their consumption, albeit at a reduced level. (Lump-sum payments, on the other hand, would normally be used - at least in part - for a one-time increase in consumption.) The effect of periodic benefit payments is to contribute to lifetime (throughout periods of sickness and throughout retirement) stability of consumption by workers and their dependants.

Social security programmes which are financed on the pay-as-you-go (PAYG) system redistribute contribution income by transferring it to households where the income of the wage earner has ceased due to the occurrence of a contingency covered by the scheme. Such schemes thus help to maintain aggregate demand and consumption, particularly if unemployment is among the contingencies covered, and economic analysis of their impact must take into account both the contributions and the benefits.

In countries where most workers are covered by a social security scheme, governments may endeavour to use the scheme as a para-fiscal instrument for managing the economy. For example, demand could be stimulated by increasing benefits or curtailed by raising contribution rates. In fact, however, because social security schemes are normally defined by statute, the opportunity to effect such changes is limited. This is as it should be because, in a comprehensive scheme, workers and their dependants plan their lives taking into account their expectations and obligations under the scheme. While a social security scheme is dynamic and must be modified from time to time to take into account socio-economic changes, these modifications should be made only after extensive public debate and consultation. Governments have other and better means of managing the economy.

F. Savings, capital formation and investment

In programmes such as a pension scheme which generates reserves or a provident fund which accumulates contributions, consumption is deferred until retirement (or death or disability). Whether such schemes induce a decline in household savings greater than the amount contributed to them, and thus a fall in aggregate national savings, has been the subject of much inconclusive research. The assets of these schemes are part of national savings. Whether the expectation of receiving social security benefits affects the savings decisions of persons covered by a social security scheme, by inducing them to decrease their personal savings, is uncertain. The effect may be negative (if benefits are used as a substitute for savings), but may equally well be positive if benefits promote retirement and people save to supplement their retirement income.

When social security schemes are financed so that substantial reserves are created, they constitute accumulations of domestic capital which may be employed to further national development. In developing countries, these reserve accumulations occur in social insurance pension schemes and provident funds. In fact, while pension schemes and provident funds may originally have been established to promote social development objectives, the massive amounts of capital which they generate – capital which is usually invested in government securities or in para-statal enterprises – has sometimes led governments to increase contribution rates in order to facilitate the placement of government securities. Since these increases have been prompted by economic, rather than social considerations, they have generally not been accompanied by improvements in the benefits or in the schemes themselves.

In the case of provident funds, and under systems of financing social security pension schemes which follow a funding formula, investments can be made for long periods and liquidity is of minor importance, if not entirely irrelevant. These schemes amass substantial amounts of capital and they can become a major, if not the principal, financial institution in a country, particularly in developing countries. While appropriate investment outlets can be defined for these schemes, in developing countries the funds available for investment can strain the capacity of national investment instruments to absorb them in worthwhile projects. The potential fiscal and monetary impact of social security investments (and in particular of a shift in investment policy or disinvestment) mean that the investments must be coordinated with, and not conflict with, government policy. In this way the social security reserve funds can best be employed to contribute to economic growth.

There need be no incompatibility between the investment requirements of a social security scheme and a country's domestic capital formation objectives; it is possible to formulate an investment policy which meets both of these conditions. Reserves should then be accumulated to produce investment income that will permit the contribution rate to be lower than it would otherwise be, and they should be invested in projects which will result in real economic growth and gains in productivity. For example, in the form of increased direct returns from an enterprise, or indirect returns resulting from improvements in the national infrastructure (such as telecommunications, roads or medical care facilities). However, if reserve funds are utilized, directly or indirectly, to meet current government expenditures they will not increase the productive capacity of the country, and they will probably not achieve a positive rate of return for the social security fund. In essence, part of the social security contribution then becomes a tax.

Government control over the investment of social security funds does not mean that they should be used systematically to finance government deficits. When they are so used, the social security scheme should receive the market rate of interest on the funds borrowed.

Social security funds are ideal for financing long-term infrastructure projects which have a high social return and which contribute to long-term economic growth (it being understood that such an investment provides, as well, a positive real rate of return). Reliance on external borrowing can be reduced. An instrument, such as a long-term social security bond, could be established to ensure that social security funds are not being substituted for other government funds which are then used to finance a deficit. The interest rate on such a bond should be based on domestic market rates for government borrowing. Selection of a higher rate would mean the government is subsidizing the scheme; a lower rate would mean that the scheme is subsidizing a government deficit.

SOCIAL SECURITY FINANCING

MODULE 2:
PRINCIPLES OF FINANCING
AND
FINANCIAL SYSTEMS

International Labour Office - Geneva

MODULE CONTENTS

MODULE 2

PRINCIPLES OF FINANCING AND FINANCIAL SYSTEMS

UNIT 1: Flow of funds in a social security scheme

A. *Sources of financing*

The most basic questions related to social security financing are: who pays, how much, on what basis, and through which institutions. The way in which these questions are addressed depends on the objectives of the social protection system and the specific benefits being financed. If the objective is to guarantee a certain minimum level of income or standard of service for the entire population, financing from general taxation is the method often applied. Alternatively, if the objective is to replace earnings during retirement, or during working life in the event of contingencies such as sickness, disability or unemployment, then financing from contributions levied on income from employment is the method commonly used, as for example in the case of social insurance schemes.

Broadly speaking, the sources of revenue of a social security scheme can be enumerated as follows: State participation; participation of other public authorities (for example, provincial and local government); special taxes earmarked or allocated to social security; contributions from insured persons; employers' contributions; income from capital, and other receipts. The decision as to the sources to be utilized and the distribution of the charges between the various sources is not purely a technical one, but has to be made on the basis of a series of economic, social and political considerations. This does not mean that the technician has no role to play in the determination of the sources of financing. On the contrary, the technician has to provide all the necessary bases so that the authorities are able to make their decision in possession of all the important elements.

Although, in an economic sense, compulsory social security contributions are a form of taxation, and in some countries are referred to as "payroll taxes," a distinction is usually made between financing from general tax revenues and financing from contributions.

Financing from taxation

Taxation may be based on personal income, capital, profits or consumption (for example, value added tax). In this regard, the financing of social benefits is part of the budgetary process, under the control of Parliament, and social security is one of the components of the larger category social expenditure, including education and health. However, some countries earmark certain taxes specifically for social security expenditure, for example, a tax on tobacco that is used to finance health services.

General revenue financing is most often associated with universal benefit schemes, i.e., benefits paid to all residents. Examples include the universal old age pensions in Canada, Denmark and New Zealand, sometimes known as "demogrants," as well as the national health services in the U.K. and Italy. Social assistance benefits (which are subject to a means test) are also financed from general revenues. These benefits are an expression of solidarity at the national level, based on the rights of beneficiaries as members of the community. Thus in many countries, the provision of medical care, children's allowances and support for low-income persons are financed from the public budget.

It is argued that social protection systems financed from taxation are better at alleviating poverty than social insurance schemes. This is because benefits are usually flat rate and are paid to people who have little or no attachment to the labour force or have limited capacity to make contributions. The impact on income distribution, and in particular redistribution between generations, is more short-term and transparent since payments to current beneficiaries are financed by taxes paid by the current population. However, universal systems are costly and thus the cash benefit amount is usually low. The Australian social security system, financed from general taxation, is categorized as a social assistance scheme, since all benefits are means tested. The targeting of benefits through a means test allows a higher rate of benefit to be paid for the same level of expenditure than in universal schemes. Unlike other social assistance schemes, the means test is set at a level which excludes only high-income earners.

Financing from contributions

When the financial resources, used to pay benefits, are collected from employers and employees covered by social security schemes, and the benefits the worker receives are based on his or her payments, the amounts are called contributions. Contributions differ from taxes in that contributions go towards increasing the worker's own benefits. Taxes are used for general expenditures of the government and the worker's payments do not affect the level of benefits the worker receives. In some cases, the State may also contribute to the scheme either according to a formula or with a subsidy, for example, to cover any deficit. If the source of funds is employer and employee contributions (i.e., no financing from general revenues), the scheme is said to be self-financing. Contributions may be either flat rate or earnings related. In many cases, if they are levied on earnings, a ceiling and/or a threshold is applied. In most contributory schemes, the record of contributions forms the basis of eligibility for benefits.

Fig. 4:

"... People are more willing to pay Social Security contributions than taxes ..."

It is often stated, as an advantage of contributory financing, that people are more willing to pay social security contributions than taxes; therefore, the potential revenue for social security expenditure is higher. Contributory schemes are supported by public opinion because contributors perceive a link between their contributions and benefits. On the other hand, contributory schemes sometimes require complex systems for determining and collecting contributions. The requirements for record keeping also lead to higher administrative costs, in particular when benefits are paid on the basis of past contributions.

Both these methods of financing are incorporated into ILO international labour standards. For example, the Social Security (Minimum Standards) Convention, 1952 (No. 102), provides that "the cost of the benefits provided in compliance with this Convention and the cost of the administration of such benefits shall be borne collectively by way of insurance contributions or taxation, or both, in a manner which avoids hardship to persons of small means and takes into account the economic situation of the Member and of the classes of persons protected." Provident funds and other schemes in which contributions are placed in individual accounts, i.e., where there is no pooling of resouces, do not, as a result, meet this requirement of Convention No. 102.

Variations in the respective shares of contributions, taxes, income from capital, and other sources, in social security financing differ from one country to another. It is also not uncommon to find different schemes in one country financed by different methods, according to the branch and the persons covered. While financing from payroll contributions is still by far the most frequently used method for cash benefits for income replacement, there has been a trend towards increasing the use of general revenues for the financing of family benefits, health care and basic pensions, particularly in industrialized countries.

B. Financial organization of a social security scheme

The financial organization of a social security scheme covers all the ways in which a scheme receives and administers the income which it subsequently disburses in the form of benefit payments and administration expenses. The topic includes the selection of an appropriate financial system and the investment of any funds which are surplus to a scheme's immediate requirements. The effective management of the various elements in the financial organization is an essential component of a successful social security scheme.

A social security scheme must be financed so that benefit payments can be made as they fall due, and administration expenses can be paid. The primary objective of the financial organization is to ensure that this condition of solvency always exists.

In order to maintain public confidence in the scheme, and to avoid economic dislocations, it is necessary that benefits be set at levels which can be supported by the contributors and that the rates of contribution to the scheme remain stable over long periods of time. In a new social security scheme, it is especially important that the contribution rates be set at levels which will not create an undue burden for the contributors and lead to adverse reactions to the new scheme.

As a result of the way in which typical systems of financing social security benefits operate, a new contributory social security scheme (particularly one offering pension benefits) initially builds up a surplus from the excess of the contributions it receives over its expenditures.

The potential social and economic implications of the investment of these surpluses must be assessed before the appropriate financial organization can be determined. The impact of these investments on the national economy depends on the nature of the economy and its capacity to absorb these surpluses in productive investments which are appropriate for social security schemes.

Cash flow in a typical social security scheme

The benefit structure (that is, the types and levels of benefits and the conditions pertaining to their payment) and the financial organization of a social security scheme are interdependent. Figure 5 illustrates the flow of funds in a typical social security scheme. The diagram provides a framework for analysing the financial operations of a social security scheme even if a particular social security scheme may not contain all the elements of income or benefit expenditure indicated.

Figure 5: Flow of funds in a social security scheme

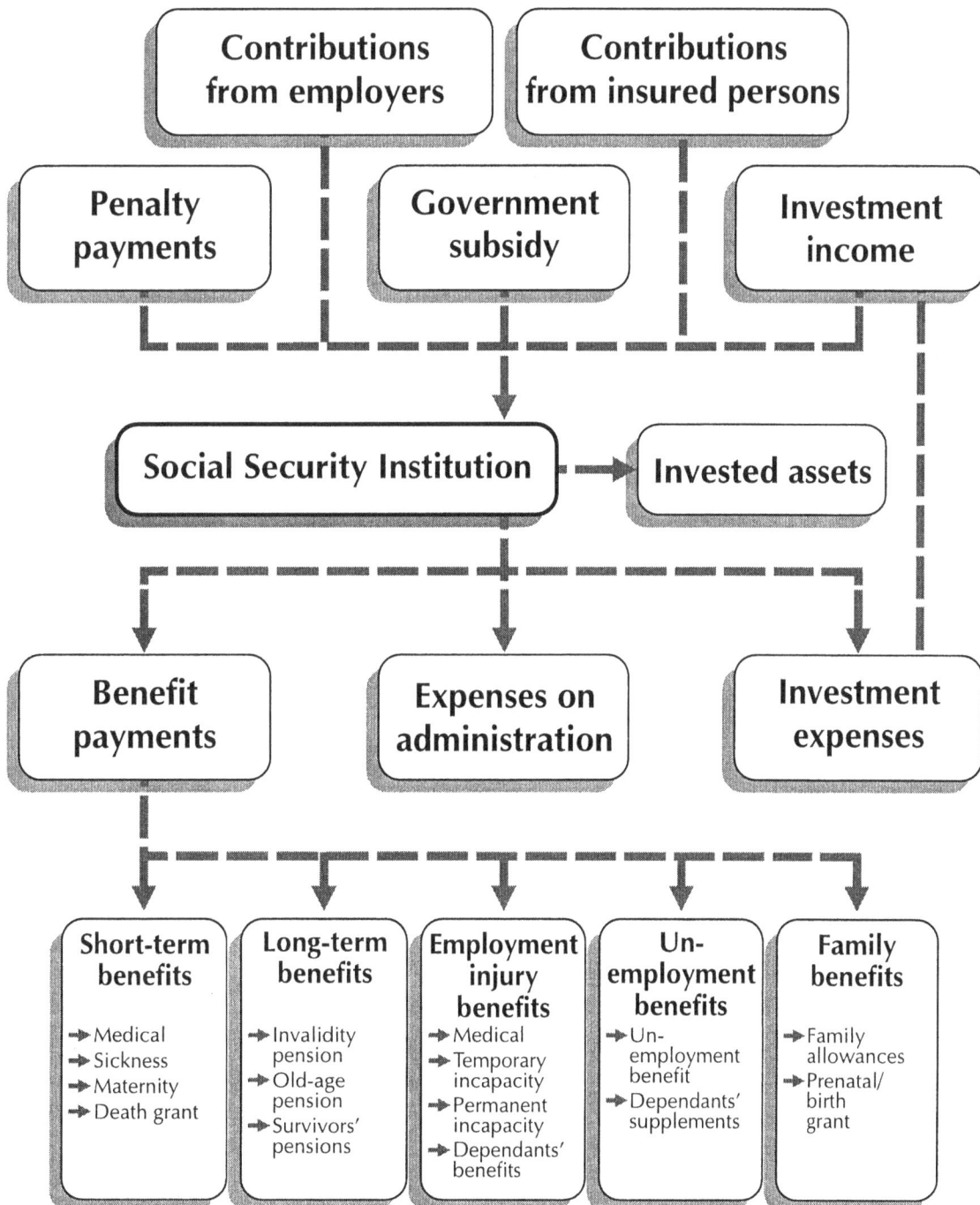

Short-term benefits	Long-term benefits	Employment injury benefits	Un-employment benefits	Family benefits
→ Medical → Sickness → Maternity → Death grant	→ Invalidity pension → Old-age pension → Survivors' pensions	→ Medical → Temporary incapacity → Permanent incapacity → Dependants' benefits	→ Un-employment benefit → Dependants' supplements	→ Family allowances → Prenatal/birth grant

Income

Generally, social security schemes receive contribution income from both insured persons and their employers. Income may also be derived from special taxes levied to support the social security scheme. The government may also make a contribution related to insured persons' or employers' contributions (or both), it may make a payment related to expenditures on certain benefits or on administration, or in some cases even a general subsidy. Normally, the government guarantees to make funds available should the income of the scheme be inadequate to meet its expenditures.

Contributions to a social security scheme may be of a uniform amount or they may be related to workers' wages or salaries, or to classes of wages or salaries. The basis for determining contributions is not solely determined by financial considerations. It depends on the types of benefits included in the scheme and on social, economic, and political factors.

The invested assets of pay-as-you-go social security schemes are an unimportant source of income because the assets accumulated are relatively small and are used primarily to provide benefits during economic downturns. In funded schemes, however, the invested assets are an important source of income.

Another source of income is the penalties assessed against employers who fail to observe the regulations of the scheme. Ideally, there would be no income from this source.

Expenditures

The expenditures of a social security scheme may be divided into benefit payments, investment expenses and expenses on administration. Benefit payments are a statutory obligation of the scheme. Investment expenses are generally assessed separately. If the coverage of a scheme is limited to certain categories of workers, expenses on administration should be met from the income of the scheme and not from general government revenues. In this way those persons who will benefit from a scheme pay its costs.

Expenses on administration comprise a category of expenditures over which management can exercise effective financial control. The regulations of the scheme may stipulate a ceiling for expenses on administration, or they may be established in the annual budget. With regard to controlling expenses on administration, it is important to consider not only the level of these expenses and their trend over recent financial reporting periods, but also the quality of the administrative services provided by the scheme. The expenses on administration are readily assessed from the financial statements and they may be analysed according to expenses on account of specific benefits, or expenses on account of specific transactions. The quality of the administrative services provided is much more difficult to assess.

It is reflected by (for example) the average time required to process a benefit claim and the number of complaints received from insured persons.

Expenses on administration are affected by both the age and the size of the social security institution. New social security institutions tend to have higher administrative expenses as they go through a learning process as to how to operate most efficiently. Small social security institutions tend to have higher administrative expenses, relative to contributions, because they cannot fully take advantage of economies of scale that arise with greater specialization of administrative functions and the ability to spread the fixed costs of administration over a larger number of participants.

C. Concepts and systems of social security financing

Social security financing can have different conceptual bases. In some countries one might seek a substantial horizontal redistribution of income. Others might limit themselves to strict risk pooling. Generally the financing concept is defined by:

- the definition of the nature of the social security system (i.e. insurance scheme or savings scheme);

- the determination of the primary financial source (i.e. contributions or taxes) or the specific mix of sources;

- the actual type of the contribution applied;

- the level of contributions.

Once the decision on the first two elements is made, it is the specific type of contribution that determines the nature of redistribution. The level or method for the calculation of contributions is directly related to the choice of the financial system of the social security schemes. Different types of contributions, and different financial systems, are discussed in the following sections.

Types of contributions

When describing contribution types we may distinguish mainly between uniform (flat) rates and wage- or income-related rates. The uniform rates are fixed at the same amount for all insured persons having the same characteristics but irrespective of the wages or earnings of the insured person. The rates may vary according to various criteria such as sex, age, region, etc. The system of uniform rates is generally applied when the benefits are also fixed at uniform rates.

The system of uniform rates is simple to understand and relatively easy to administer. However, it should be noted that this system includes a regressive element as the percentage of the wage, represented by a flat-rate contribution, is the greater with smaller wages and vice versa. This regressive character is more important the greater the spread in wages. Consequently, it is desirable to fix the rate at a modest level in order to avoid too heavy a burden on the lower-paid workers, or to fix the contributions at reduced rates for this category of worker. This system is mainly applied under schemes aiming at providing a minimum level of subsistence and is not appropriate for schemes which aim at a level of protection related to the standard of living of insured persons.

The contributions fixed in relation to wages or income are determined either as a percentage of wages or income, or by classes of wages or income. The system of wage- or income-related contribution rates is generally applied when the benefits are also fixed in relation to wages or income. However, this is not always the case. There are schemes where the benefits are fixed at flat rates but where the contributions are wage or income related, in which case the contribution takes the character of an income tax and would normally lead to substantial redistribution of income.

In general, both where the contributions are fixed as percentages of wages or income and where they are fixed by classes of wages or income, a ceiling is applied. The part of the wages or income exceeding the ceiling is not taken into account for the calculation of contributions. The ceiling for contributions is generally the same as the ceiling applied for the calculation of benefits, but there are schemes which apply different ceilings for the two purposes. For example, if the ceiling for the calculation of benefits is relatively low compared with the ceiling for the calculation of contributions, then the scheme approaches those referred to, where the contribution takes the character of an income tax or a special tax. Where a ceiling *is* applied, it is important not to fix it at too low a level as it would not take into account an important part of the wages or incomes of the insured persons; in fact the scheme would approach the system of uniform contribution rates. On the other hand, if the ceiling is fixed at a very high level, it does not have any meaning and is practically superfluous. The ceiling should also be adjusted to take account of increases in wages or income; in many schemes this is done on an annual basis.

The method of fixing the contributions by classes of wages or income is, to some extent, a combination of two systems: the system of uniform rates and the system where the contributions are fixed in a direct proportion (or percentage of) wages or income. Normally, with higher wages or income, the contributions will be higher and in this respect the system of wage classes is analogous to the system of directly proportionate contributions. However, the two methods differ by the fact that the system of wage or income classes may include a regressive or progressive element. For example, the contribution for each class can be fixed in such a way that it represents a higher proportion in the higher wage classes and a lower proportion in the lower wage classes, thus providing for a progressive contribution assessment; similarly a depressive effect is obtained by the opposite procedure.

The method of wage or income classes in fact represents a system of uniform contributions for the different levels of wages. If the number of classes is small, and the interval of each class is great, the relative importance of the contribution may vary rather substantially, within each class, in such a way that the contributions for those insured persons whose wages approach the lower limit of the class represent a heavier burden than for those whose wages approach the upper limit. On the other hand, for the purpose of simplifying the administration, it is preferable to have as small a number of classes as possible. In establishing the wage classes, therefore, two requirements have to be reconciled; namely equity in the burden of contributions, and simplicity in administration. As in the case of the adjustment of the ceiling, the wage classes should be indexed.

The distribution of the contributions is also an issue covered by international labour standards. Specifically, Convention No. 102 provides that "the total of the insurance contributions borne by the employees protected shall not exceed 50 per cent of the total of the financial resources allocated to the protection of employees and their wives and children. For the purpose of ascertaining whether this condition is fulfilled, all the benefits provided by the Member in compliance with this Convention, except family benefit and, if provided by a special branch, employment injury benefit, may be taken together." In practice, there is considerable variation between countries, but in many countries the contributions are divided equally between employers and employees.

Financial systems and the determination of contribution levels

One of the most important technical questions that is posed in connection with the financing of a social security scheme is which financial system to apply. Systems of finance, in relation to social security programmes, are the methods by which funds are allocated in order to provide the expected benefits as they fall due. The financial system is also the method by which the financial equilibrium, between receipts and expenditure, is ensured. The advance funding of benefits may be at a high or low level, or there may be none at all, in which case certain benefit expenditures may be met out of the current income of the social security institution. The appropriate system of finance, for a particular benefit, depends principally on the nature of the benefit. Additional important considerations include: the scope of coverage (that is, the proportion of the population covered by the scheme); the advisability or necessity of maintaining reserve funds; the investment opportunities for these funds; the need to retain relatively stable contribution rates; and the need to establish contribution rates which do not prove burdensome to employers and insured persons. In the case of a scheme which is already in operation, the maturity of the scheme must also be considered.

Fig. 6:
"one of the most important questions ... is ...
Which financial system to apply ..."

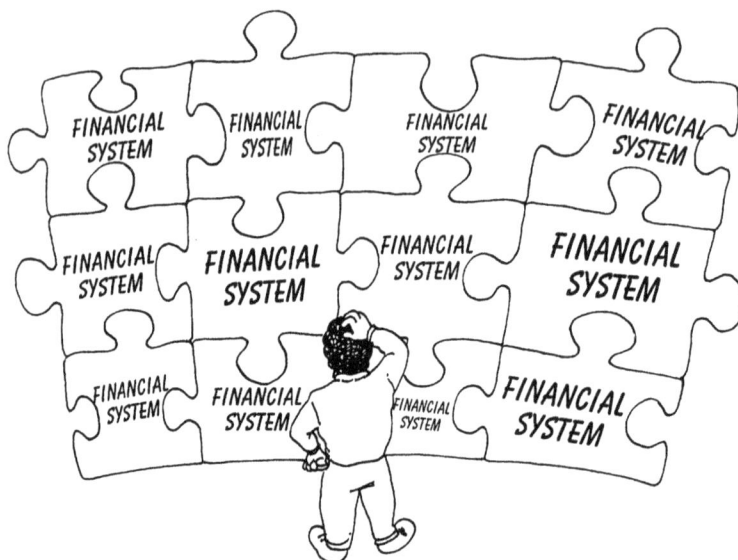

There are many systems of finance which could be employed to finance social security benefits. In practice, a few systems - which may be regarded as model systems - are commonly used.

Mixed systems are also found where a benefit, or a class of benefits, is financed utilising more than one system of finance.

The system (or systems) of finance which are to be followed in a particular social security scheme may be stated in the law, or in the regulations of the scheme, or the matter may be left to the discretion of the scheme's board of directors. In order to provide a firm but sufficiently flexible basis for defining the systems of finance which are to be applied, the matter should normally be dealt with in the regulations.

An actuary estimates the amounts which will be required to pay benefits in the future, but the exact amounts cannot be stated because unforeseeable changes will occur. For example, changing demographic patterns will affect the numbers and durations of pension payments, or an epidemic may lead to a larger number of sickness benefit claims than was estimated. Because exact estimates are impossible, funds known as contingency reserves must be set aside to meet unexpected increases in the numbers and value of benefits payable. The appropriate levels of the contingency reserves for the various social security benefits will depend on the types of benefits and the contingencies which may cause variations in the amounts payable.

The method for the calculation of the contribution rate in social insurance schemes is usually determined by national law. The law is usually concerned with maintaining the financial solvency of the scheme and, basically, has to oblige the management of the scheme, or a legislative body, to adjust the contribution rates when the financial resources of the scheme are considered insufficient. Hence the law defines a decision making rule as to when the contribution rate has to be changed.

In other words, the legal provisions would stipulate that whenever financial projections are made, then the projected reserve should not be lower than a certain funding level (referred to as "k") during a defined period of equilibrium of (x) years.

It is crucial to signal the time when a change is necessary, and when a new required contribution level has to be set. This is usually done by defining the "actuarial equilibrium" of a scheme. The actuarial equilibrium is a discretionary concept closely related to the chosen financial system for the individual branch of social security. The actuarial equilibrium could be defined by a simple provision in the law which states:

> "The reserve of the scheme at the end of each calendar year (t) within a period of X years has to amount to at least k times the benefit expenditures (or total expenditure) in year t-1"

The actual determination of X and k determines the level of funding of the scheme, as well as the financial system. The value of k could be smaller than one, and x equal to one, which would describe a pay-as-you-go scheme with a small contingency reserve. A bigger k indicates that the scheme is at least partially funded. There is a wide variety of rules applied internationally: in the US, for example, k is relatively high and x equals 75 years; whereas in Germany, k is smaller than 1 and x is only 15 years.

In analysing the systems of finance of social security benefits it is convenient to consider short-term and long-term benefits as separate branches. Employment injury benefits, which have characteristics of both short- and long-term benefits, are also considered as a separate branch. This analysis is confined to compulsory social insurance schemes. Provident funds, which are essentially compulsory savings schemes and do not involve a pooling of risks, are discussed separately.

The following sections deal with the determination of contribution levels under the different systems of financing. To provide a rough and preliminary overview on the typical size of the contribution rates in one branch of social security, old-age, invalidity and survivors' benefits, Table 1 summarises the experience in selected countries.

Table 1: Contribution rates for old-age, invalidity and survivors' benefits in selected countries, 1997

Country	Employer (% of payroll)	Employee (% of earnings)
Austria	12.55	10.25
Bahamas*	5.4	3.4
Canada	2.7	2.7
Cameroon	4.2	2.8
Germany	9.3	9.3
Ghana	12.5	5.0
Greece	13.33	6.67
Japan	8.25	8.25
Jordan	8.0	5.0
Malaysia**	12.0	10.0
St. Vincent	3.0	2.5
Trinidad & Tobago	5.6	2.8
USA	6.2	6.2
Zimbabwe	3.0	3.0

*For insured earnings above certain level   **Provident fund

Source: U.S. Social Security Administration, **Social security programs throughout the world - 1995,** Washington, D.C., 1995.

UNIT 2: Short-term benefits

A. What are the benefits included in this category?

Short-term benefits include medical care, cash benefits for sickness and maternity, unemployment benefits and death grants. Family benefits, although they are generally payable for longer periods, may also be included in this category. Short-term benefits, which are payable for a limited period (generally not more than one year), are characterized by an ultimate annual expenditure which is relatively stable when expressed either as a proportion of the total annual insured earnings or as an average amount per insured person, since over a period of years the annual frequencies and average durations of these benefits are relatively stable.

B. Which is the financial system for short-term benefits?

A financial system which recognizes these characteristics of short-term benefits is the pay-as-you-go (PAYG) or annual assessment system. Under this unfunded system, contributions in respect of the benefits are set at such a level that, in any year, the contributions (plus any investment income earned on the contributions) will be adequate to meet the benefit expenditures and the expenses on administration incurred in the year. In order to maintain stable contribution rates, a small margin is added to the contribution rate and the funds arising from this margin are held in a contingency reserve.

C. The determination of contribution rates in the short-term benefit branch

The contribution rates to finance short-term benefits may be determined either a priori or a posteriori. In the former case, a provisional contribution may be fixed at the beginning of the year, which is then adjusted at the end of the year according to the actual experience during the year. This procedure is used mainly in mutual benefit societies, in respect of sickness and maternity benefits, and sometimes also in respect of other benefits, such as death or burial benefits. If the contribution rate is fixed a posteriori, the employers and the workers will not know in advance the amount which they will have to pay as a definitive contribution. This can have an influence on the economic and financial measures they would like to take for the year concerned. Therefore, the system of predetermining the contribution rate is increasingly being used. This means that the contribution rate is fixed, in advance, on the basis of actuarial estimates based either on previous experience of the scheme or on experience drawn from other schemes. The contribution rate thus arrived at should include a margin of safety permitting the establishment of a contingency reserve to absorb non-foreseeable variations and occasional fluctuations in expenditure. It is, of course, important that the contribution rate is fixed in such a way that it can be kept stable for as long a period as possible without fixing it at too high a level. There are thus two conditions which operate in opposite directions. In order to find the most satisfactory solution, the contribution rate should be determined on the basis of carefully prepared actuarial calculations and analyses executed with great caution.

It is very important that the financial regulations of the scheme contain precise provisions for fixing the rate of contribution; in other words the period of equilibrium, both for the initial period and for successive periods. They should also prescribe, in detail, how to determine the time for modification of the contribution rate.

In its most simple form, the basic formula for the financial equilibrium of a social security scheme is written:

Receipts = Expenditure	(or Income = Outgo)

and, where the rate of contribution is predetermined, the formula is written:

Probable receipts = Probable expenditure

where probable expenditure is equal to

Probable benefit expenditure + Probable administrative expenditure.

The objective of the actuarial estimates is therefore, in the first instance, to establish the probable annual benefit expenditure. This may be done either by estimating the global amount or, if the contribution rates are fixed in proportion to wages, the estimates often aim at establishing the relative cost which is the annual benefit expenditure related to the total annual amount of wages on which contributions are assessed.

In order to illustrate the various elements which enter into short-term benefit calculations of this kind, it may be useful to quote a simple formula for the calculation of probable benefit expenditure.

If there is only one type of benefit this formula is written as follows:

$n \times f \times m \times k$, where

$n =$	number of persons exposed to risk (= number of insured persons);

$f =$	frequency of occurrence of the risk;

$m =$	average number of days per case of risk;

$k =$	average cost per day.

For example, in the case of daily sickness cash benefits f denotes the number of cases of sickness compensated during the reference period (in our case a year) per insured person; m denotes the average number of sickness benefit days per compensated case, and k denotes the average amount of benefit per compensated day of sickness.

$n \times f$
is the estimated total number of sickness cases to be compensated during the year.

$f \times m$
is the morbidity rate, which is the average number of sickness benefit days per insured person per year.

$f \times m \times k$
is the average cost of sickness benefits per person per year.

$n \times f \times m$
is then the total number of benefit days to be compensated during the year.

and finally, the product $n \times f \times m \times k$ is the total probable cost of daily cash sickness benefits for the year.

Elements used in the actual calculation will depend on the form in which data is available. Often, for example, tabulations are available showing the morbidity rates. From this, the average cost of cash sickness benefit, per protected person, per year, can be obtained simply by multiplying by factor k.

Certain refinements in the basic formula could be introduced by subdividing the protected persons into more homogeneous groups, for example, by age, sex, geographic region, etc. For each of the sub-groups, the factors entering into the formula (the f, the m and the k) have to be determined separately and the partial results added. The statistics available do not always permit following these more refined methods and often the estimates have to be made globally.

While it is only necessary for actuarial estimates to have the product $f \times m \times k$, or the average cost of sickness cash benefits per protected person per year, it is very useful to know the value of each factor in order to be able to analyse, separately, each factor's effect on the cost of the benefits and to assess the variations in the total cost when modifications are made in one or other of the basic hypotheses for the estimates or in the benefit provisions.

In order, therefore, to obtain appropriate actuarial bases for the establishment of financial estimates, social security schemes should compile statistics on each component and, if possible, the breakdown by age, sex, geographic region, occupation and also by main cause of sickness.

It is also important to distinguish between the various components in order to make comparisons with experience from other countries and, if necessary, to be able to use data drawn from foreign experience for one or another of the components. Caution must be exercised, however, when using data drawn from foreign experience. Each of the elements entering into the formula is influenced by a series of factors peculiar to each scheme, for example the legal provisions governing qualifying period, waiting period, benefit period as well as the level of benefit as compared with the general level or wages of the protected persons, etc. It is interesting also to note the lower morbidity rate in agriculture than in industry and that there can be substantial differences between the various regions within a country. For some of these factors adjustment can be made by means of so-called reduction or elimination tables, particularly in so far as waiting period and maximum benefit period are concerned.

These differences may, to some extent, reflect real variations in the incidence of sickness, but certainly other factors play an important role. It is clear that the frequency rate is influenced by social, economic and other factors which may act differently according to regional conditions. Among such factors could be mentioned the ratio of benefits to wages and the volume of unemployment; experience shows an increase in compensated sickness during periods of unemployment. Another important factor is the standard of certifications of incapacity by physicians.

Sickness benefit

The following simple example illustrates the use of the formula in a sickness benefit scheme which pays 50% of the daily wage for each work day a covered worker is absent due to sickness:

Assume:

n = 100,000 insured persons
(morbidity rate) = $f \times m$ = 8 days

average annual wage = s = 1200
Assuming there are 300 work days per year, then
the average cost per day
k = 0.50 $\times$ 1200/300 = 2

Then, total annual cost = $n \times f \times m \times k$ = 100,000
$\times$ 8 $\times$ 2 = 1,600,000

Total annual wages subject to contributions = $n \times s$ = 100,000 $\times$ 1200 = 120,000,000

Hence, relative cost

= total annual cost/total annual insured wages
= 0.0133 = 1.33% of insured wages.

This result could, of course, be obtained by working directly from the formula for relative cost, namely:

$$\frac{n \times f \times m \times k}{n \times s}$$

where k in this case is equal to 0.5 $\times$ s/300 which inserted in the formula gives

$$\frac{n \times f \times m \times 0.5 \times s/300}{n \times s}$$

which can be reduced to

$f \times m \times 0.5/300$ = 8 $\times$ 5/300 = 0.0133 or
1.33 per cent.

It should be stressed that this figure expresses the estimated relative cost and cannot be used directly as a contribution rate as, for example, administrative cost has not been taken into account. Furthermore, depending upon the reliability of the basis for the calculations, it is necessary to add a margin of safety, in order to absorb unforeseen variations in the various elements which entered into the formula, or a margin to be built up of the minimum contingency reserve required by the legal definition of the actuarial equilibrium. If it is a new scheme, where the elements are not drawn from the experience of the scheme, one has to be particularly prudent. First, if the estimates have been based on statistics available on absenteeism in establishments, these statistics are influenced by a series of factors which do not apply to a new scheme; so that it cannot be assumed that the data represent the morbidity which a social security scheme will have to face. For example, the level of benefit for temporary incapacity granted by the establishment, if the establishment provides such benefits, as compared with the benefits provided by the social security scheme, the attitude of the individuals towards the benefits under the scheme, the certification and possibilities of control of temporary incapacity, as well as a series of other factors. All such factors have to be taken into account when assessing the basic data for actuarial estimates.

What is also important is the fact that, in a new scheme, experience shows that the morbidity is low during the first years before the insured persons have become fully aware of their rights. The morbidity rate will therefore increase gradually over a rather long period. Consequently, the experience of the scheme during the first years can not be taken as representative for the future operation of the scheme; particularly so if the scheme is being introduced in stages, by geographic regions, by industry, or by size of establishment. Under some schemes the fact that the benefit expenditure has proved to be substantially lower than the estimates, during the first years, has led the authorities to raise the benefits. Later, when the operation of the scheme has reached complete application, the receipts may then no longer be sufficient to cover the expenditure and it will be necessary to have recourse either to an increase of contributions, to subsidies from public funds, or to a reduction of benefits. These measures do not inspire confidence in the scheme and one of the most important conditions for the success of a scheme is that it has the confidence of the parties concerned, that is the workers and the employers.

Maternity benefit

To give another example, consider the cost of maternity cash benefits, assuming the scheme provides daily cash benefits at the same rate as the sickness benefit to all insured women employed in covered establishments. The maximum benefit period may be assumed to be six weeks before and six weeks after confinement, or a total of 12 weeks. The total cost of this benefit depends, in the first instance, on the proportion of women in the insured population. Let us assume that this proportion is 20 per cent. For the frequency of the contingency or number of maternity cases per insured woman, we assume a figure of 0.1 or, on average, one birth per ten insured women per year. In so far as the average duration of benefit is concerned, experience shows that in practice the benefits are not paid for the maximum period for all beneficiaries. There are cases of premature births, abortions, delayed cessation of employment before birth, etc., where the benefit period will be shorter than the legal maximum. Therefore, if the maximum is 12 weeks we can assume a shorter average benefit period, say 10 weeks. The value of m is consequently 60 days when assuming the benefits are payable only in respect of work days.

In the example of cash sickness benefits the estimates were based on an average daily wage of 4 (1200/300) which, at the 50% benefit rate, gave rise to a benefit of 2 per day. However, wages for women are generally on average lower than wages for males. For k, the average cost per day, we may assume that the average wages for women are 80 per cent of those for all insured persons giving a value of k = 1.60 per day (0.50 x 0.80 x 1200/300).

The total cost is consequently:

$$100,000 \times 0.2 \times 0.1 \times 60 \times 1.60$$
$$=$$
$$192,000 \text{ monetary units.}$$

When related to the total annual wages subject to contributions, 120,000,000 monetary units, the relative cost is 0.0016 or 0.16 per cent of insured wages.

Medical care benefits

A third example concerns medical care benefits. Medical care benefits are services. In general they consist of: general practitioner and specialist care; supply of pharmaceuticals and other medicaments; hospitalization; x-rays and laboratory tests; transportation of sick persons; physiotherapy treatment; etc. Consequently, the cost of medical care benefits is not directly related to an insured person's earnings.

To illustrate the applicable principles for the establishment of actuarial estimates, medical care benefits can be grouped into four types of expenditures, and estimates for each type made separately. The expenditure groups are:

- care by medical practitioners (medical consultations);
- supply of pharmaceuticals;
- hospitalization;
- other care.

The estimates of cost of care by medical practitioners, as well as the other benefits, depend on the methods by which the benefits are provided, in other words, whether the social security body runs its own medical services or if the care is provided by the public health services; or if the care is given by doctors under special contracts and paid, for example, by the number of patients treated; or if the care is provided by private practitioners on a reimbursement basis.

It is necessary to stress the importance, for the estimates, of the differences in procedures for providing medical care. Medical care may be provided by the social security organization's own medical care facilities, or by the public health services, or both. If the estimates relate to a scheme not yet in operation, the necessary data are not available, but one can often draw some data from foreign experience. For example, the number of consultations per protected person shows a certain regularity and, if the selection is made carefully, one can obtain reasonably reliable estimates. If, for example, we make the assumption that the average number of consultations in respect of a protected person (i.e. including the insured person and his dependants) per year is ten, then $f \times m = 10$, and if we assume that the average cost per consultation is 1.5, then the total cost of medical consultations would be $100,000 \times 10 \times 1.5 = 1,500,000$. In the example the relative cost would consequently be 1.25% of insured wages $(1,500,000/120,000,000)$.

In so far as the other medical care benefits are concerned we may proceed in the same way. For pharmaceuticals the data have to be very carefully analysed, as statistics for this benefit are influenced by a multitude of factors which must be taken into account in practice (e.g. availability, access, pricing, distribution system). As an illustration, assume that the number of prescriptions per protected person per year is 5 and the cost per prescription is 1. The total cost will consequently be $100,000 \times 1 \times 5 = 500,000$ and the relative cost would be 0.42% of insured wages.

In so far as hospitalization is concerned, the estimate may be based on the average number of cases of hospitalization (f in the formula), the average duration of hospitalization per case (m in the formula), and the average cost per day of hospitalization (k in the formula). However, the morbidity rate ($f \times m$), the average number of days of hospitalization per protected person is often used. If we assume that the morbidity rate is 0.75 and the daily cost of hospitalization is 10, the total cost of this benefit will be $100,000 \times 0.75 \times 10 = 750,000$ and the relative cost is 0.63% of insured wages.

Finally, for the item "other care", let us suppose that, on the basis of a detailed analysis of all the various services provided under this heading, the estimate of the relative cost of other care is 0.3% of insured wages.

The total relative cost of benefits according to the example is:

Sickness cash benefits		1.33%
Maternity cash benefits		0.16%
Medical care benefits:		
Medical consultations	1.25%	
Pharmaceuticals	0.42%	
Hospitalizatio	0.63%	
Other care	0.30%	2.60%
		———————
Total relative cost		4.09%

To this would have to be added administrative expenses, which may vary substantially from one scheme to another and from one country to another, so that it is not possible to provide any standard figure. However for purposes of the exercise to illustrate the procedures, we may assume that the relative cost of administration amounts to 0.6% of insured wages.

The total relative cost is consequently 4.69% of insured wages. For the determination of the contribution rate to be applied, a number of other factors have to be considered. For example, as mentioned earlier, if the scheme is new and the basis for the estimates is not very solid, the margin of safety must be of some importance. If the scheme needs to build up and extend medical facilities, it will be necessary to take this into account in determining the contribution rate.

Finally, it should be stressed that the calculations presented here are meant only to illustrate the general methods followed, and to indicate the importance of keeping adequate statistics and accounts which permit the calculation of the various elements which, in turn, form the basis for the actuarial estimates and actuarial analyses.

UNIT 3: Long-term benefits

A. What are the financial systems?

In most countries the financing of the pension insurance scheme poses the most complex problems. It can be said that it is the most important social security branch from an economic, perhaps also social, and even political, point of view. In any case it is this branch, in particular, which gives rise to political debate in various countries. As numerous financial systems are used for pensions schemes, it is not possible to examine all of them in detail. What follows, therefore, is a brief description of the most basic systems, namely the PAYG system and the general average premium system, as well as certain intermediate systems.

Long-term benefits include old-age, invalidity and survivors' pensions. These benefits are normally payable for longer periods than are short-term benefits, and additional factors must be considered in the selection of an appropriate financial system for them.

Long-term pension benefits have a future expenditure pattern which is quite different from that of short-term benefits. The following factors generally contribute to a pattern of annually increasing expenditures on pensions (1) in absolute terms, (2) in proportion to total annual insured earnings and (3) as an average amount per insured person:

- Each year a new group of insured persons, or their dependants, qualifies for pensions. This results in annual increases in the number of pensions in payment for many years after the inception of the scheme.

- Pension benefits generally increase with the years of service of the insured person at the time the benefit becomes payable and, the longer a pension scheme operates, the greater will be the average years of service applied to determine new pension benefits.

- When the pension is based on an insured person's earnings, at or near the time he/she qualifies for a pension, the average annual pension will generally increase each year.

- Beneficiaries of pensions awarded in previous years will continue to receive pensions and, because longevity generally increases, future pension beneficiaries will receive them for increasingly longer periods.

- Pensions already in payment may be increased in accordance with increases in the level of wages or cost of living.

B. The contribution rates under different financial systems

U nder a pension scheme the total amount of pensions will, as a rule, increase year by year over a rather long period. The moment when the scheme has reached stability or maturity depends on a series of factors of demographic and economic nature as well as on the legal provisions governing the scheme. The evolution of such a pension scheme can be illustrated by a curve (Figure 7) increasing rather steeply to begin with but gradually levelling out.

Under the unfunded PAYG system of finance, no funds would be set aside in advance, and the benefits under a pension scheme would be paid from current contributions. Given the pattern of rising annual expenditures in a social insurance pension scheme, if the PAYG system were applied, the contribution rate (as a percentage of insured earnings) would be low at the inception of the scheme and would increase annually for many years thereafter.

Figure 7: Contribution rates under different financial systems

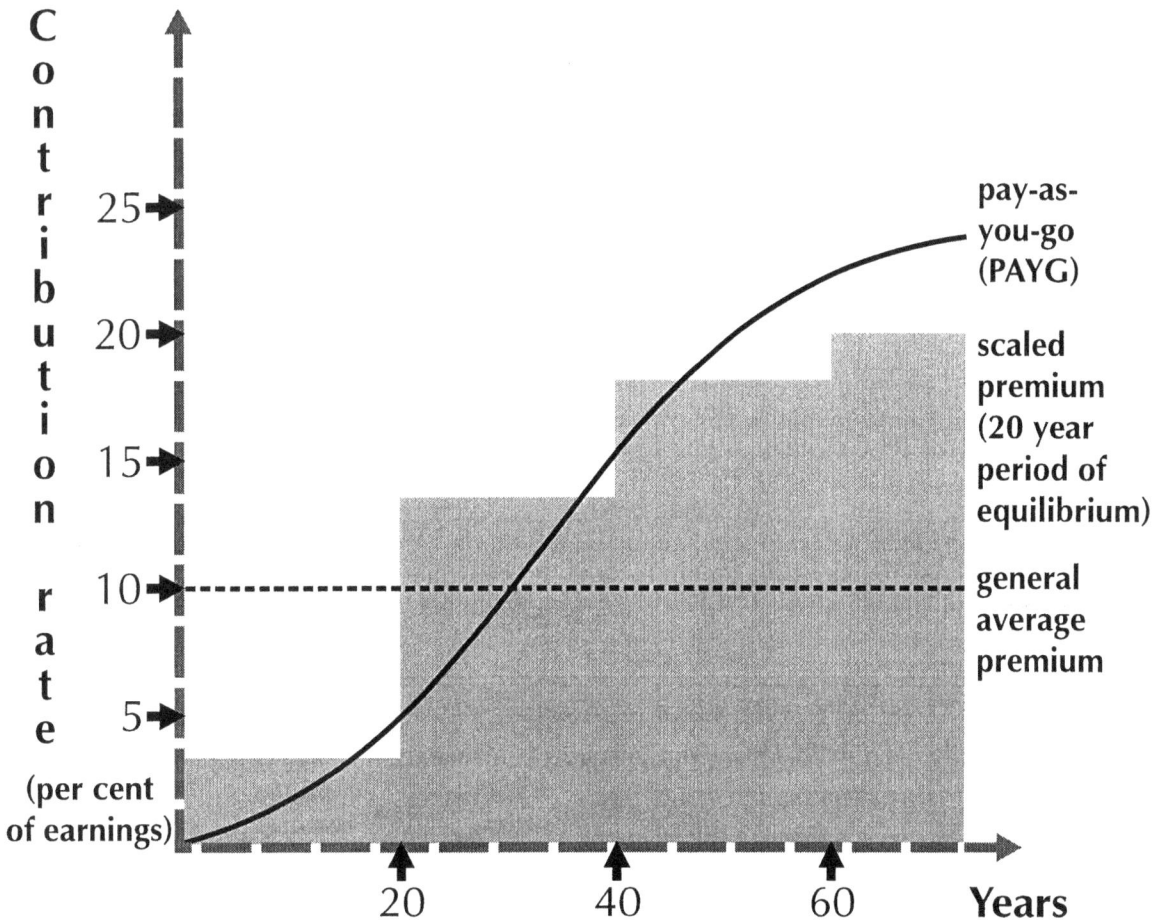

At the other extreme, a contribution rate which theoretically remains constant indefinitely may be calculated by setting:

the present value of estimated future expenditures on pensions and administration	= factor x	the present value of estimated future insured earnings.

(*Present value* means the amount, at a point in time, of future payments taking into account expected future interest rates and the probability that the persons in respect of whom the payments will be made will survive to make, or receive, the payments.)

Both elements in the equation are estimated for existing insured persons and for future new entrants to the scheme. (Any existing funds of the scheme are deducted from the disbursement side of the equation). Solving for the factor gives an estimated annual contribution rate, as a proportion of insured earnings, which would in theory be adequate to meet the disbursements of the scheme for an indefinite period. This financial system is referred to as the *general average premium* system. Figure 7 also shows the contribution rate (i.e. general average premium) which would apply under this system.

The contribution rate established by this system is a fixed proportion of annual insured earnings. Since, in a typical social insurance pension scheme, annual disbursements in respect of long-term benefits are an increasing percentage of insured earnings, and since the contribution rate is set at a level to ensure indefinite financial equilibrium between the income and disbursements of the scheme, it is evident that in the early years (and generally for many years) the contribution rate will exceed the rate which would apply under the PAYG system. Consequently, during this period, the annual contribution and investment income of the scheme will exceed its annual disbursements. This excess forms a technical (or actuarial) reserve which is invested, and the interest thereon supplements contributions income when annual disbursements eventually exceed the annual contributions based on the general average premium system of finance.

C. Actuarial calculations, estimates and assumptions

Whether the indefinite financial equilibrium, which the general average premium financial system is designed to achieve, actually materializes depends largely on whether the actuarial assumptions, on which the calculations are based, are realised. While the PAYG system requires actuarial estimates to be made for a period of one year (or at most a few years), the general average premium system requires assumptions for a period which can extend several generations into the future.

The dynamic factors which the actuary must estimate, include:

- demographic factors such as:
    - mortality;
    - morbidity;
    - increases in the number of insured persons;
    - proportion of persons married;
    - average age difference between spouses;
    - average number and ages of children;

- economic factors such as:
    - interest rates;
    - wage levels and scales by age;
    - cost-of-living adjustments in wages and pensions.

It is evident that assumptions which will remain valid indefinitely cannot be made with a great degree of confidence. The actuary endeavours to make realistic assumptions and to provide safety margins in some assumptions to offset potential deficiencies in others. It would, of course, be possible to make assumptions as to variations of the different elements, for example decreasing mortality, and this is sometimes done. But there are a series of other elements for which it is difficult to make any assumption as to future variations and, even if one could make such assumptions, the number of possible calculations would multiply so quickly that it would be difficult to draw any valid conclusions.

In this connection it may be interesting to note that, for a pension scheme providing old-age, invalidity and survivors' pensions, the selection of the mortality basis generally has a minor importance for the total cost, because the effect of mortality works in opposite directions in respect of old-age pensions and in respect of survivors' pensions. In a social insurance pension scheme, particularly in a new scheme where there is little experience on which to base the assumptions, they are unlikely to remain valid throughout the long period necessary to establish the general average premium contribution rate. Hence both the assumptions and the contribution rates must be reviewed periodically.

Actuarial calculations can be made either on the assumption of "closed fund" or "open fund". In the first case it is assumed that the scheme will always be limited to the initial population, whereas in the second case new entrants into the scheme in the future are taken into account. The method of closed fund is usually applied for schemes of limited coverage, such as occupational pension schemes for individual undertakings. It would be unrealistic to assume that there would be no future entrants to a social insurance scheme. The assumptions regarding future entrants are, however, difficult to make because they relate both to number and age composition, as well as the wage structure, of each batch of future entrants. The assumptions concerning future entrants to a social security scheme have an important influence on the general average premium.

D. *Characteristics of the general average premium and the scaled premium financial systems*

General average premium

The *general average premium* system has certain characteristics which render it unsatisfactory for financing social insurance pension schemes. In a new scheme, the contribution rate will be substantially higher than the contribution rate under the PAYG system and it may be too high for workers and employers to afford. The substantial reserves which are generated under the general average premium system may also exceed the capacity of a national economy to absorb them productively.

The system is very useful for making comparisons of cost between different options. For example, if the authorities would like to know the consequences of different pensionable ages, or different solutions for recognition or crediting of years of service prior to the entry into force of the scheme, the actuary can easily calculate the general average premiums for the various options. This permits the authorities to make their decision on the basis of the relative financial importance of the different alternative solutions.

Increases in the cost of living have an adverse effect on old-age, invalidity and survivors' pensions, and in order to maintain the real value of pensions in payment it is necessary to increase them from time to time to take account of such changes. When inflation is high, such adjustments must be made more frequently than annually in order to maintain the real value of benefits. Generally, cost-of-living adjustments based on price changes provide lower increases than adjustments based on wage changes.

In a funded scheme, the reserves which are held in respect of future benefit payments must also be increased whenever the pensions in payment are increased, and the higher the level of funding of the scheme the greater are the funds required in order to meet the increase in reserves. Consequently, under the general average premium system, the adjustment of pensions in payment is most difficult because substantial increases in the reserves (from investment or contribution income or both) are necessary.

In private occupational pension schemes, the systems of finance are comparable to the general average premium system, and lead to the accumulation of substantial reserve funds. This is considered necessary in order to protect workers accrued pension benefit rights against the possibility that the employer may at some time cease operations resulting in the pension scheme being terminated. The high level of funding means that, even if the employer ceases operations, the worker will still receive the accrued pension benefits arising from the period of service with the employer. Since social security schemes are not subject to premature cessation, and since they normally have a continuous flow of new entrants, it is not necessary to have a high level of funding in order to guarantee the promised benefits.

For the reasons set out above, the general average premium system is rarely used to finance social insurance pension schemes. It is useful principally to indicate the probable long-term cost of a pension scheme. In mature social insurance pension schemes, where the age distribution of the population has attained a degree of stability, financial systems approaching the PAYG system are usually applied. For a new social insurance pension scheme, or one which has not yet reached a mature state, the annual increases in the contribution rate which would occur make the PAYG system unsuitable, and an alternative system of finance is generally used.

Before considering other possible options, it is important to emphasize that the total expenditure, and the incidence of expenditures, in a pension scheme depend on the benefit structure and the characteristics of the persons insured under the scheme. The actual expenditure is entirely independent of the financial system, which simply determines the level of funding applied to the scheme and the manner in which funds are made available to meet expenditures.

A system of finance suitable for a social insurance pension scheme should meet several criteria.

- The contribution rate should not exceed the capacities of insured persons, employers and the economy in general to support it.

- The reserves generated should not exceed the capacity of the country to effectively absorb the investments in a profitable manner.

- Contribution rates should remain relatively stable for extended periods of time, and any increases should be gradual.

There are an infinite number of options for intermediate financial systems which satisfy the above criteria. For example, the financial system could be defined by the requirement that the contribution rate be set so that, at the end of any year for a specified number of future years (e.g. 20), the reserves of the pension scheme are at least equal to a specific multiple (e.g. two times) of the pension benefits expected to be paid, and expected expenses on administration, in the next year.

Scaled premium

A more sophisticated financial system which can meet the above-noted requirements, is the *scaled premium* system. This system has been characterized as particularly suitable for financing long-term social security benefits in developing countries.

Under the scaled premium system, a contribution rate is established so that, over a specified period of equilibrium (for example 10, 15 or 20 years), the contribution income and interest on the reserves of the scheme will be adequate to meet expenditures on benefits and administration. This is, in effect, a specific definition of an actuarial equilibrium. There are various ways to define specific scaled premium systems using different definitions of the actuarial equilibrium. One of the systems frequently used by the ILO is the scaled premium system that provides for a non-declining reserve throughout the period of equilibrium. Under this definition, during a period of equilibrium, those reserves which have arisen during previous periods (from excesses of income over disbursements) are not required to meet expenditures of the scheme, so they may be placed in long-term investments. The contribution rate, during the initial period of equilibrium, will lie between that which would apply under the PAYG system and the general average premium system. The scaled premium financial system has the following characteristics:

- A period of equilibrium is chosen which is of limited duration but is sufficiently long to guarantee a certain stability of the contribution rate.

- The contribution rate is determined in such a way that the expected receipts (contributions and investment income) of the scheme, during the period of equilibrium, will be equal to expected expenditures.

- The financial system does not provide for the use of the principal of the accumulated funds to cover current expenditure (only the interest on the accumulated funds is used).

- When current contributions, plus investment income, are no longer sufficient to cover expenditure, the premium is raised to the level required for a subsequent period of equilibrium.

The longer the period of equilibrium, the higher is the contribution rate and the greater the accumulation of reserve funds. The scaled premium system permits flexibility in establishing the contribution rate and controlling the amount of the reserve funds which a scheme will generate, while still committing the scheme to a methodical financial system. In order to avoid a decrease in the reserves, the contribution rate must be revised *before* current receipts fall short of current expenditures.

Until a scheme reaches a mature state, increases in the contribution rate must occur from time to time in any social insurance pension scheme which follows a system of finance other than the general average premium system.

This means that the pensions of one generation of workers are paid, in part, from the contributions of succeeding generations of workers. The extent of this inter-generational transfer depends on the level of funding (the higher the level, the lower the transfer) and the maturity of the pension scheme. Under a scaled premium financial system, any necessary increases in the contribution rate are made gradually, based on recommendations arising from actuarial valuations of the scheme. Under a scaled premium system, the period for which actuarial assumptions must be made is limited, they may therefore be made with reasonable precision, and any increases in the contribution rate can be managed so as to avoid abrupt changes and possible economic dislocations.

The scaled premium system (or any other intermediate financial system) is not a means of reducing the cost of pension benefits. It is an orderly, yet flexible, system of setting aside funds to meet benefit and administration expenditures. Initially it produces a lower contribution rate, and a lower rate of accumulation of reserve funds, than would apply under the general average premium system. The flexibility, which the scaled premium system provides, enables it to adequately meet the criteria which apply to financial systems for new social insurance pension schemes. Figure 7 (on page 51) indicates the typical relationships between the contribution rates under all these systems: the scaled premium system (with a 20 year period of equilibrium), the PAYG system and general average premium system.

E. Special topics in pension scheme financing

As the financial aspects of pension schemes are generally more important than for the other branches of Social Security, it is of interest to look in some detail at elements inherent to the scheme, as well as outside it, which can have an important influence on the cost of the scheme and its financing. The provisions governing the scheme are obviously of primary importance, particularly those relating to the rate of benefits, qualifying periods, pensionable or retirement age, definition of invalidity, definition of survivors, transitional provisions, provisions for crediting of previous service, and so on.

Pension age

The pension age plays a crucial role in determining the cost of a pension scheme. For example, the cost of pensions payable from the age of 55 can be double (or even more) than the cost of pensions payable from the age of 65. The pension age has to be fixed in the light of a series of considerations such as: the general working capacity of aged people; the situation of old people in the labour market; the economic possibilities of financing pensions; etc.

Very often, in the discussion of the pension age, reference is made to life expectancy but this mortality measure is frequently used in a wrong sense. The "expectation of life" indicates the average number of years which remain for persons who have attained a given age, if they are subject to the mortality conditions for the period covered by the life table concerned. Reference is often made to "expectancy of life at birth". This means the average number of years which remain for the new born if they are subject to the mortality conditions expressed by the mortality table. It is well known that, in nearly all countries in the world, there has been a substantial improvement in mortality but this improvement is particularly due to a reduction of mortality of infants and young persons. If a comparison is made between the countries having a heavy mortality and those where the mortality is light, in general it would be found that the mortality in the younger age groups is substantially higher in the countries of the first category than in those in the second category. For the older age groups, however, the mortality in countries in the first group tends to approach that in the second group. It is dangerous to fix the pension age at a relatively low level when basing the argument on considerations of a low figure for expectancy of life at birth. What is important, and must be balanced from benefit adequacy and cost points of view, is life expectancy at the upper ages.

Transitional provisions

Transitional provisions are applied when initiating a new social insurance pension scheme, or when changing from one type of scheme to another; for example from a provident fund to a pension scheme. In the case of social insurance, transitional provisions are intended to permit persons, who have attained a certain age at the entry into force of the scheme, to be able to draw a pension even if they would not satisfy the normal conditions for a full or partial pension. Such provisions are often combined with others which govern crediting of service prior to the entry into force of the scheme. The financial effect of such provisions depends, of course, on how they are formulated. For example if, under the provisions, all periods of service prior to the entry into force of the scheme are to be credited, the pensions resulting from the application of these provisions have to be paid. Generally, it will be impossible to re-establish the entire period of service for a relatively long period of, say, 30 to 50 years. The financial importance of such provisions can be considerable. They can double, or even triple, the cost, depending on the age distribution of the insured persons as well as on the structure of the scheme concerned. Under certain schemes, particularly private schemes or schemes limited to certain occupations or industries, a special capital payment may be made to cover the recognition of previous service. However, such a payment can attain considerable proportions and, therefore, this procedure is not practicable for a social security scheme. In view of the fact that it is administratively impossible to re-establish employment careers going back for 30 to 50 years, a method of "fictitious recognition" of previous service, based on the age of the persons concerned at the date of entry into force of the scheme, is generally applied. Provisions could, for example, be formulated as follows: all persons who have been insured for the first year of operation of the scheme are entitled to be credited with a certain number of insurance periods, in relation to their age at the date of entry into force of the new scheme; e.g. 3 or 4 months for each year of age exceeding a specified age (say 25 or 30) subject to a certain maximum (say 120 or 144 months). The financial consequences of such provisions are relatively easy to determine.

Fig. 8:

" ... It is of interest to look ... at elements ... which can ... influence cost ... and financing ..."

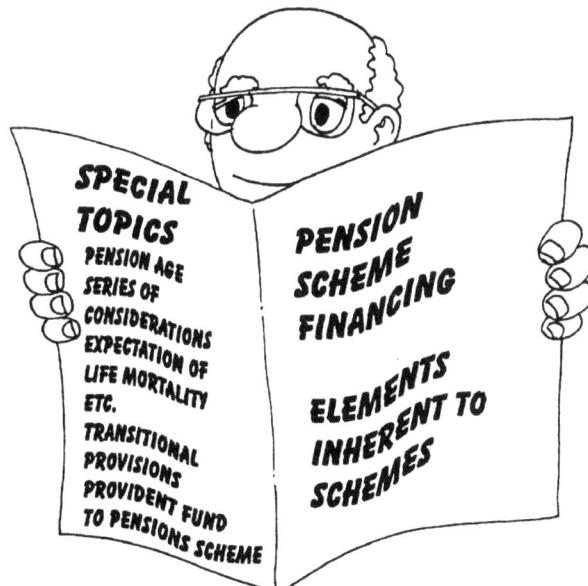

F. *Provident fund benefits and mandatory retirement saving schemes (MRS)*

The systems of finance which have been outlined are applicable to social insurance schemes where (i) there is a pooling of risks and contributions, and (ii) the benefit (which is normally in the form of periodic payments) is related to an insured person's earnings at or near the time the benefit becomes payable (and often to the period of covered employment). A provident fund, where the amount of the benefit is whatever lump-sum amount has accumulated in the member's account at the time the benefit is payable, follows a system of full funding on an individual basis.

Mandatory retirement savings schemes (MRS) are a variant of the provident fund system which have recently attracted some interest, notably in Latin American countries.

Under MRS schemes the balance of the savings account, at time of retirement, is converted either into:

- an annuity (i.e. monthly payments) on a strictly actuarial basis; or
- monthly "programmed" withdrawals (i.e. scheduled de-savings) from the balance.

The conversion into an annuity consists of the division of the balance by an annuity factor which reflects:

- the remaining expectation of life (i.e. taking into account mortality rates after the age of retirement);
- expected interest rates;
- and (sometimes) the expected rates of future inflation adjustments of the monthly payments.

Programmed withdrawals are a schedule of withdrawals, from the savings accounts, which has to follow certain rules.

In stable economic environments these schemes may provide old-age benefits which are sufficient to maintain a decent standard of living *only* after a relatively long savings period. For the first two to three decades, at least, the retirement income generated by the saving schemes may have to be supplemented from other sources. In view of the general uncertainty of long-term economic developments, and the related risks for any savings scheme, all social protection schemes that rely on individual savings have to be safeguarded by government guarantees, underwritten by the general budget. In Chile, where this system was first introduced in the 1980s, the Government guarantees a minimum pension level. The system also needs additional special insurance arrangements for the contingencies of invalidity and survivorship – as it cannot provide sufficient protection to workers, or their families, in case of early invalidity or death.

UNIT 4: Financial administration

A. Separation of accounts

Most social security schemes provide a combination of short-term, long-term and employment injury benefits, and sometimes also operate a provident fund. Since different systems of finance apply to each of these benefit branches, separate accounts of income and expenditure must be maintained for each branch, and the funds accumulated in each branch must be separately recorded. During periodic actuarial reviews, these accounts and records are examined to determine whether the contribution rates, established for each branch, are appropriate and whether the actuarial assumptions are being realized. Under the financial system being applied, the contribution rate established for each branch should be adequate to permit the branch to be self-supporting. A deficit in one branch should not unwittingly be met from funds contributed or allocated to another branch. For example, a deficit in the short-term branch (financed by PAYG) which cannot be met by drawing on the contingency reserve for this branch should not be met by a transfer from the reserve funds of the long-term branch, unless there is full recognition that this method of meeting the deficit is being used and means are devised for replenishing the long-term reserve. Failure to operate the branches in this manner can result in meeting current deficits at the risk of incurring a serious short-fall in the reserves of the long-term branch at some time in the future.

B. Expenses on administration

The expenditure of a social security scheme may be divided into benefit payments, investment expenses and expenses on administration. Benefit payments are normally a statutory obligation of the scheme. Investment expenses are generally assessed separately and deducted from gross investment income. The expenses on administration comprise a category of expenditures over which management is able to exercise effective financial control. The regulations of the scheme may stipulate a ceiling on expenses on administration, or they may be established in the annual budget approved by the board. The chief financial officer must monitor the expenditures on administration in the periodic statements of account and thereby maintain control over this aspect of the scheme's operations.

In its efforts to control expenses on administration, management must consider not only the level of these expenses and their trend over recent financial reporting periods, but also the quality of the administrative services provided by the scheme. The expenses on administration are readily assessed from the financial statements and they may be analysed according to expenses on account of specific benefits, or expenses on account of specific transactions. The *quality* of the administrative services provided is much more difficult to assess. It is, hower, reflected by items such as the average time required to process a benefit claim, the number of complaints received from insured persons, etc.

Sophisticated techniques for analysing expenses on administration may be introduced. Expenses which are directly related to a measure of workload may be analysed by cost per transaction; the trend of the resulting ratios can be observed over time. If the expense per transaction tends to rise over the period of observation, it may be inferred, other things being equal, that the unit responsible for the transaction is becoming less efficient, i.e. that it is costing more to process each transaction. However, this apparent decrease in the unit's efficiency may have resulted from improved service which the unit is providing to insured persons and beneficiaries. Cost and service aspects must, therefore, be considered together.

The expenses on administration which are likely to be incurred in the coming financial period must be estimated in the annual budget. These expenses should be estimated on the basis of the amounts which will reasonably be required to administer the expected contribution income and benefit expenditures plus senior management, actuarial, external auditing and other expenses, including overheads which are not directly related to the scheme's income or expenditure. This approach to budgeting expenditures on administration gives management's best estimate of the expenses *which are likely to be incurred.* It is preferable to budgeting expenses on administration on the basis of the maximum amount *which it is estimated will be available* to be spent on the administration of the scheme.

After the board has approved the budget, management must endeavour to operate the scheme, during the financial period, within the approved limit on expenses on administration. Should it subsequently appear that the budgeted limit on these expenses will be inadequate, it will be necessary to ask the board to approve expenditures in excess of the limit.

In order to permit effective financial management and to ascertain the administrative expenses of each social security branch at the end of the financial year, all the expenses of administration must be allocated among the branches. Sophisticated formula to effect this allocation may be devised.

However, it may be undesirable to require extensive records to be kept (which itself creates an expenditure) in order to make the allocation. A simple formula may be devised which is based on the assumption that expenses on administration are related to the total contributions and benefit payments, in each branch, during the financial period. This formula will give an approximate allocation of the expenses on administration in each branch. In the financial period let:

> L = the total contribution income and benefit expenditure for the long-term branch,

> S = the total contribution income and benefit expenditure for the short-term branch,

> E = the total contribution income and benefit expenditure for the employment injury branch,
> and
> A = the total expenses on administration for all branches.

Then the approximate expenses on administration for each branch in the financial period can be computed as follows:

$$\text{Long-term Branch Admin. Expenses} = \frac{L}{L+S+E} \times A$$

$$\text{Short-term Branch Admin. Expenses} = \frac{S}{L+S+E} \times A$$

$$\text{Employment Injury Branch Admin. Expenses} = \frac{E}{L+S+E} \times A$$

An analysis of the administration expenses of each branch is conducted by the actuary during his valuation and should be undertaken by the board and management after each allocation. The ratio of the expenses on administration, in a branch, to the contribution income of the branch in the same period, should be calculated; the trend of these ratios, over successive financial years, should be examined.

ANNEX: *Employment injury benefits*

Broadly speaking, there are two major types of scheme for employment injury benefits: namely, employer's liability schemes, where the benefit entitlement is based on the individual liability of the employer to provide the benefits, and the schemes based on the principles of social insurance. In some countries, where the scheme is based on the employer's liability, the law only stipulates the liability of the employer but does not require any financial guarantees; whereas, in other countries, the law requires certain guarantees for future liabilities. This guarantee may be in the form of compulsory insurance with private companies or mutual societies. Very often a public insurance institution is established to regulate the insurance market in this field and to take the risks which are not accepted by the private insurance companies. Often, such a public insurance institution also acts as a supervisory authority for the scheme.

In schemes which are based on the principle of social insurance, the risk of employment injury has to be insured compulsorily with a public insurance carrier, or institution, or the liability for benefits is assumed directly by the State. The insurance may be carried out by a special institution administering only the branch of employment injury, or it can form a special branch of a general social security system. Finally, the employment injury insurance, instead of constituting a separate branch, may be integrated in a general scheme so that the benefits in respect of employment injury are provided under other branches, such as the sickness branch and the pension branch. Under this type of scheme there is evidently no particular problem of financing the employment injury benefits. However, very often there are special provisions applying to employment injuries, for example in respect of the qualifying period, higher benefits or special supplements and special benefits such as protheses or special care. In these cases the financing of employment injury benefits may pose particular problems.

Employment injury schemes which provide medical care and temporary incapacity cash benefits, as well as permanent incapacity and survivors' pensions, include both short- and long-term benefits. Employment injury benefits are generally financed only by employers and are usually treated as a separate branch of social security.

PAYG is the financial system normally used for employment injury temporary incapacity benefits and medical care benefits, as well as for any lump-sum payments, and the annual cost of rehabilitation and accident prevention programmes.

The permanent incapacity and survivors' pensions, under employment injury schemes, are like the invalidity and survivors' pensions in the long-term branch. However, the incidence of these pensions is relatively low, and eligibility for a pension, and the amount of a pension, are independent of a worker's period of employment at the time the worker becomes an invalid or dies. Funds are not normally set aside, in advance, to pay the pensions which are likely to arise from death or incapacity due to employment injury. Instead, the contribution rate is set so that, in any period (usually a year), the income of the scheme will be sufficient to meet all the employment injury benefit payments to be made in respect of injuries incurred during the period.

The *terminal funding financial system* (or system of assessment of constituent capitals) is normally used to finance these pensions. The system involves the capitalization of future benefit payments. Under this system, a calculation is made of the present value of each new employment injury pension, at the time it is awarded (i.e., the value of all future pension payments is estimated at that time); this amount is then transferred from the contributions to the employment injury scheme in the year to a *technical reserve* for employment injury pension benefits. Each year thereafter, the reserve is credited with interest at the rate assumed in calculating the present value (assuming this rate is not greater than the net rate of interest actually earned in the year) and debited with the amount of pension payments made in the year. The objective of this technical reserve is to serve as a guarantee for the payment of future pensions; the reserve is not intended to be spent at short notice. The funds can, therefore, be placed in long-term investments.

Setting contribution rates

The contribution rates may be fixed either prospectively or retrospectively. In the latter case, a provisional contribution is paid at the beginning of the year (or in the course of the year) and, after the year end, an adjustment is made according to the claims experience during the year. This procedure is frequently applied when differential rates, and merit or experience rates, of contributions are applied. Alternatively, the contributions may be predetermined by estimates based on previous experience, without having recourse to any adjustments - except in exceptional cases, or where the expenditure is exceeding receipts in such a way that the resulting deficit cannot be absorbed by the contingency reserve. Obviously, this system requires good statistics which permit close following of the evolution of the scheme, enabling the competent authorities to take action at the appropriate moment. It also requires that the reserve funds are maintained at the level provided for in the financial regulations.

Employment injury reserve funds

An employment injury social insurance scheme would have two reserve funds, each with very different objectives. There is the *technical* (mathematical or actuarial) *reserve*, which serves as a guarantee for the pensions in course of payment. At the end of each financial year, the reserve fund must be at least equal to the capital value of all pensions in payment. The calculation of this reserve is made on the basis of actuarial tables, either individually by beneficiary or by groups of beneficiaries.

Then there is the *contingency reserve* for the employment injury branch. The objective of this reserve is to meet any unexpected excess (chance variation) of expenditures over receipts, in order to maintain the contribution rate at a stable level. Contrary to the technical reserve, it is not possible to forecast when funds from the contingency reserve may be required. The contingency reserve funds must, therefore, be held in liquid assets.

The following is an illustration of the operation of the employment injury technical reserve. It also demonstrates the principles of the terminal funding system. The examples are necessarily rather simple and the hypotheses and assumptions are extremely simplified.

Assume that, at the end of a financial year, there are three male invalidity pensioners, A aged 25 years with an annual pension of 1000, B aged 45 years with a pension of 2000 and C aged 55 years whose pension is 3000. Suppose also there is one widow pensioner, D aged 55, whose pension is 1000, and one orphan C aged 6, who can receive an annual pension of 200 until age 16.

Actuarial tables give the present value of annuities payable in the future, according to the age of the annuitant. A table of annuities for invalids gives the following values for males: age 25 - 13.3; age 45 - 11.8; age 55 - 9.9. An annuity table for females gives the value 15.8 for age 55. From a table for annuities payable up to age 16, the factor is 8.2 for the age of 6 years.

Consequently, the technical reserve would be:

Invalids:	A: 1,000 x 13.3	= 13,300 units
	B: 2,000 x 11.8	= 23,600 units
	C: 3,000 x 9.9	= 29,700 units
		66,600 units
Survivors:	D: 1,000 x 15.8	= 15,800 units
Orphans:	E: 200 x 8.2	= 1,640 units
	Total:	84,040 units

The technical reserve, which is equal to the capital value of the pensions in payment, is then 84,040 units at the end of the financial year.

Of course, such small numbers of pensioners are not encountered in practice. (In fact, the smaller the number of beneficiaries, the more variation may be expected in the various elements entering into the calculations, and the greater must be the margin of safety in the calculations.) The procedure followed would normally be by age groups. For example, all beneficiaries of an invalidity pension would be grouped by age, the amount of pensions totalled for each age group, and the total multiplied by the value of the annuity for the age concerned. By adding the results for all age groups, the total amount of the technical reserve fund, which should figure in the balance sheet, is obtained.

Rating systems

Up to this point, the questions of financing have been dealt with in a global way without considering the distribution of charges among the various categories of insured persons. In general, this question does not arise in other social security branches, but in the employment injury insurance branch several systems exist for fixing the contribution rates or premiums. To some extent, this has resulted from the historical evolution of this branch, from schemes based on employers' individual liability to schemes based on the principles of social insurance. The question of which system to use for fixing contribution rates or premiums is raised, particularly, in countries which are transforming their schemes from employers' liability to social insurance schemes.

In general, three different systems, for fixing contribution rates under employment injury insurance schemes, can be distinguished: *uniform rates, differential rates* by industry or by class of risk, and *merit or experience* rates.

Uniform rates

Under the system of *uniform rates*, the contribution rates are fixed without taking into account the risks or hazards in the establishment or undertaking, or in the industry to which it belongs, or the activities which the establishment carries out.

The system of uniform rates has the advantage of being simple to apply. Once the contribution rate is fixed, the assessment of contributions may be made in the same way as for the other social security branches. It also has the advantage that the collection of contributions can be coordinated, or combined with, the collection of contributions for other social security branches; this represents a substantial saving in administration. It also subtsantially simplifies the work of employers.

One objection to the uniform rates system is that it does not encourage employers to observe safety measures and regulations as do other systems, particularly the system of merit or experience rating. However, in most countries which apply the system of uniform rates, the legislation contains provisions under which the insurance institution can impose increases in the contributions, or claim reimbursement of benefits, from employers who have infringed safety rules or failed to introduce safety measures. Accident insurance institutions can also be made responsible for the promotion and enforcement of accident prevention.

Differential rates

There are great variations in the incidence of employment injuries among industries and establishments. Under the system of *differential rates*, each establishment is assigned to a class according to the activity which it carries out, or according to the branch of industry to which it belongs. Contribution or premium rates are then fixed for *each* risk class or industry. No account is taken of the accident experience of the individual establishment, nor of any measures taken for accident prevention. When the criteria for classification of an establishment change, for example due to a change in activity or production, the establishment is assigned to the class to which it belongs under the new conditions and the contribution rate for the new class will be payable.

Under the system of differential rates, each class is usually considered as an autonomous financial unit. Statistics and accounting data are compiled separately for each class, which permits the fixing of the contribution rate which will be sufficient to assure the financial equilibrium of the class. The contribution rates under this system are subject to periodic reviews.

Supporters of differential rates argue that the system of uniform rates does not provide for an equitable distribution of charges among the various industries and establishments. This raises the basic principle of the extent of collective solidarity in social security. For other branches of social security (such as, for example, sickness and unemployment) the incidence of the contingency varies quite substantially from one group of insured persons to another. The incidence of sickness varies by age, sex, occupation, geographical region, etc., and in some schemes, particularly those based on voluntary or private insurance, the contribution rate may vary according to these factors. However, in most compulsory social insurance schemes, the principle of collective solidarity is observed and uniform rates, independent of any risk factors, are applied.

In employment injury insurance, which in most countries has developed from individual employer's liability through private insurance to social insurance, the principle of collective solidarity in fixing contribution rates has not been generally established. It is true that the variations of the incidence of employment injury by industry or occupation are generally higher than for other branches of social security.

To what extent is it justified that there be a relationship between the incidence and cost of a contingency and the charges to be borne by or on behalf of the various groups of the insured population?

Compared to the system of uniform rates, the application of differential rates requires a more complex administrative machinery. Statistical and accounting data must be available by risk class in order to enable reviews of the contribution rate fixed for each class. The system requires qualified and experienced staff for classification of the establishments, as it is often difficult to draw a clear-cut line between the different classes. The question of classification becomes more difficult as the number of classes increases.

Merit or experience rates

The *merit or experience* rating system is an extension of differential rating. Merit or experience rates are fixed, or adjusted, according to the accident experience in an individual establishment and/or on the basis of the accident prevention measures taken by the establishment. This system is generally applied when the employment injury insurance is operated through private insurance companies.

The system is usually based on a schedule, or classification of industries or occupations by risk, which indicates a "normal", "average", or "manual" rate of contribution or premium for each class. This normal rate can then be modified, upwards or downwards, within certain limits according to an individual establishment's accident experience, safety measures undertaken and/or the general safety conditions in the establishment. The elements which are taken into account, and the way in which this system is applied, vary greatly. For example, the limits within which the contributions can be reduced or increased, in relation to the normal rate, are usually of the order of 20 - 50 per cent of the normal rate.

The merit or experience rate system may be restricted to establishments over a certain size. The system is applied to small establishments mainly when the merit rating is made according to prevention measures taken by, or to safety conditions in, the individual establishment. When the rating is made according to experience, the application is usually limited to establishments over a certain size so that chance variations in the incidence of accidents play a lesser role and statistical data are, therefore, more significant.

The administration of a system based on merit or experience rating is elaborate. All establishments have to be classified individually; all records and statistics have to be kept individually; and highly qualified and specialized personnel are required to assess the various factors affecting the fixing of the contribution rate for each establishment. Decisions in this respect may be a source of dispute. This is especially the case for new schemes, where the necessary experience has not yet been accumulated. When the system is not yet well established, and the rules are not clear, personnel responsible for the application may also be subject to undue pressure from the interested parties. In view of the complicated administrative machinery, the merit or experience rating system will involve much higher administrative costs than the system of uniform rates. As in the case of the system of differential rates, it is difficult to co-ordinate and combine various operations, such as the collection of contributions, with other social security branches.

Arguments in favour of a merit or experience rating system are similar to those for the system of differential rates. It is contended that merit or experience rates promote accident prevention, since there can be a direct benefit to the employer from successful prevention activities undertaken in an enterprise. The rates should provide for a more equitable distribution of the charges among the various establishments and branches of industry. This raises the issue of collective solidarity in social security financing which was mentioned in connection with differential rates. It may be noted that, if the experience rating system is applied in its extreme, the insurance element (pooling of risk) would disappear and each establishment would "self-insure" (i.e., pay its own accident costs). In practice, there are limits to the adjustments below and above the "normal" rate.

Fig. 9:
"... In general ...
Three different systems for
fixing ...
Employment injury
contribution rates ..."

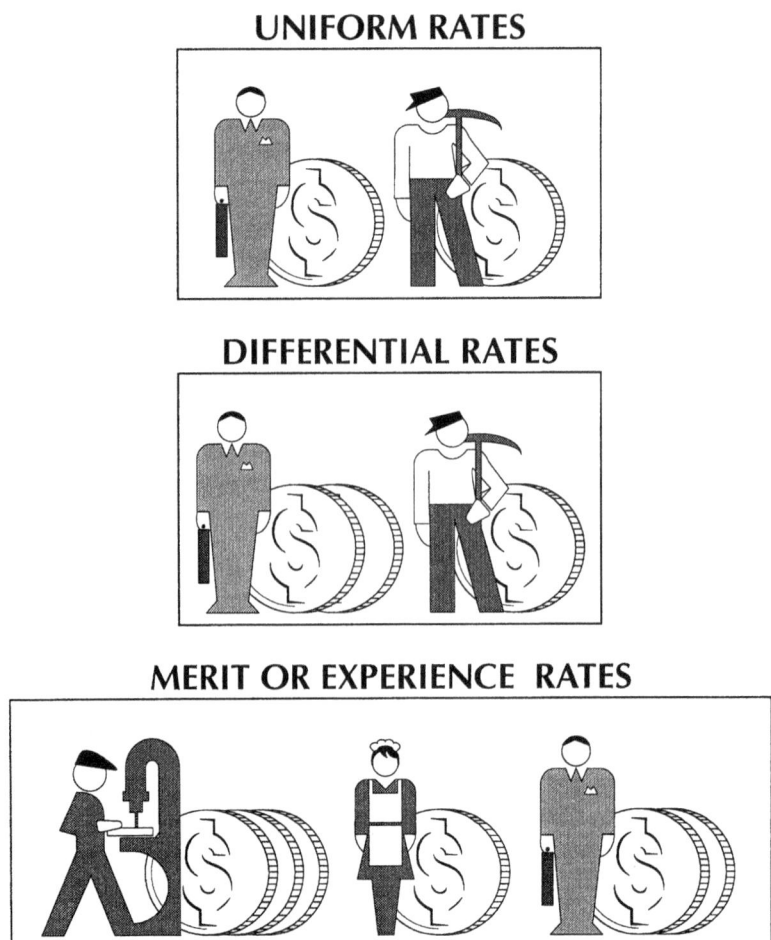

UNIFORM RATES

DIFFERENTIAL RATES

MERIT OR EXPERIENCE RATES

SOCIAL SECURITY FINANCING

MODULE 3:
ACTUARIAL AND
STATISTICAL METHODS

International Labour Office - Geneva

MODULE CONTENTS

UNIT 1:   **Actuarial valuations of
a social security scheme**

A. Actuarial valuations

B. Actuarial reports

C. Communicating valuation results and follow-up

UNIT 2:   **Data for actuarial valuations**

A. Data on insured persons and beneficiaries

B. Amount of actuarial (technical) reserve

C. Demographic and financial assumptions

D. Demographic and financial projections

UNIT 3:   **Inflation and adjustment
of benefits**

A. Effect of inflation

B. Adjustment of benefits

MODULE 3

ACTUARIAL AND STATISTICAL METHODS

UNIT 1: Actuarial valuations of a social security scheme

A. Actuarial valuations

What does an Actuary do?

An actuary is a specialist in the application of a certain kind of financial statistics. The calculations which the actuary makes are used to assess the financial consequences of future transactions which are in some way uncertain, or contingent on some kind of risk.

Fig. 10:
"... a specialist in the application of ... financial statistics ..."

APPLICATION .... OF FINANCIAL STATISTICS

FUTURE TRANSACTIONS .....

+UNCERTAINTY/

CONTINGENT ON RISK

= FINAL CONSEQUENCES

Traditionally (but not exclusively), actuaries have been concerned with demographic risks, i.e. those concerned with human life. In fact, the actuarial profession first developed (over 200 years ago) in association with the invention of life insurance as it is now known. The actuaries' calculations were needed to work out the yearly premiums to be charged for such life insurance policies, and the reserve funds which had to be maintained to ensure payment of the sums due under the policies. The calculations which are needed in relation to a pension scheme are very similar in principle, and this is a major part of the work carried out by actuaries for social security pension schemes.

The actuary's calculations thus involve a combination of:

- evaluating the contingency risk, and

- discounting, to allow for the time value of the relevant monetary payment.

In principle, every future payment may be categorised:

- in an insurance fund:
  - the income from premiums, and
  - the outgo by way of sums assured, payable when policies mature;

- in a pension scheme:
  - the income from contributions, and
  - the outgo for benefit payments, including pensions on retirement and invalidity, and to survivors of deceased members.

In addition, it may be necessary to take account of receipts of interest, dividends on investments, and expenditure on administration.

The present value of each payment can be estimated by multiplying together:

- the expected money amount of the payment

- the statistical probability that the payment will in fact be made

- the discounting factor allowing for the time at which the payment falls due.

The results of all of these calculations can be added together to estimate the actuarial assets and liabilities of the insurance fund or pension scheme.

In practice, of course, the future payments in such a scheme are likely to be extremely numerous, and the actuarial calculation of assets and liabilities will be very complicated. Historically, actuaries developed techniques for grouping the calculations so as to enable tables of special factors to be applied; in this way the calculations became much more practical. In modern conditions, however, calculations involving many components, each of them relatively simple in nature, can be carried out very rapidly using computers.

Even now, the actuarial calculations required, for example in a moderately large social security pension scheme, can strain the resources of quite powerful computers, but the use of this technology has certainly transformed the day-to-day arithmetical work of the actuary. However, the role of the actuary, in making the relevant statistical analyses and in interpreting the results of the calculations, is just as important as ever.

The financial systems considered appropriate for a social security scheme, and the initial contribution rates for the various benefits, are normally recommended by an actuary. In order to make recommendations the actuary must collect and analyse economic and demographic data pertinent to the operation of the scheme. If, as is frequently the case, these data are incomplete, unreliable or not available, the actuary must make recommendations on the basis of assumptions which are judged to be appropriate to the scheme.

When recommending the initial contribution rates, it is not possible for an actuary to be certain of selecting a set of assumptions which will be realized in their entirety. Therefore, the actuary must draw on experience and recommend a contribution rate which will permit the scheme to commence operations on a sound basis. The assumptions will be refined later in the light of statistical and financial data showing how the scheme has actually fared. It is essential, therefore, to compile statistics on the operations of the scheme regularly, both to provide management with the information needed to administer the scheme effectively, and for the purposes of the periodic actuarial valuations. These valuations, which are intended to ensure that the scheme operates on a sound financial basis, are normally statutory requirements which are undertaken every three or five years. The importance of actuarial valuations is recognized in international labour standards. Convention No. 102 provides that a government "shall ensure, where appropriate, that the necessary actuarial studies and calculations concerning financial equilibrium are made periodically, and in any event, prior to any change in benefits, the rate of insurance contributions, or the taxes allocated to covering the contingencies in question."

Actuarial valuations of social security schemes, like those of other insurance institutions which are required to have actuarial reviews, are conducted by independent actuaries (or actuaries who are obliged to adhere to strict rules of professional conduct concerning valuations of schemes operated by institutions with which they are associated). An actuarial report should include forthright comments on any matters which affect the financial status of a social security scheme. These can include: deficiencies in the design or operation of the scheme; the financial system applied; the scheme's income; the efficiency and cost of its administration; and its investment policy and performance.

An actuarial valuation is concerned with the long-term solvency of a social security scheme. Often, this long-term perspective is neither well-understood nor appreciated. The valuation assesses whether income and outgo will balance in the future under the financial system (including the contribution rate) which has been established. It is *not* concerned with verification of the accuracy and probity of the annual accounts. This is dealt with by auditors. The actuarial valuation is thus the fundamental test of the financial viability of a social insurance scheme. It indicates whether the system of finance being applied, and the planned level of contributions, can be sustained.

An actuarial assessment would most obviously be needed in the type of social security scheme in which the benefits are paid in the form of pensions. The liabilities comprise streams of cash payments which are dependant on the contingencies of death (giving rise to payments of pensions to dependants), survival (relating to pensions payable to members themselves) and of becoming disabled (assuming that the scheme in question pays pensions in such circumstances). Estimating the total value of the liabilites at the present time (or some other fixed point in time) therefore requires calculations of the type described above. Equally, the part of the assets represented by future expected receipts of contributions is also dependent on the probability that members survive to pay the contributions, and on the time value of the monetary payments.

A scheme which is purely of the provident fund type also has assets and liabilities represented by future payments whose present value is time- and contingency-dependant. However, in such a scheme the benefit payments to each individual are equal to the accumulated value, at the time of claim, of the contributions made by and on behalf of that individual. In calculating the actuarial values of overall income and future benefit outgo, the demographic and financial discounting factors effectively "cancel out", so that the actuarial values of the assets and liabilities are necessarily equal. Such a scheme is usually regarded as being automatically in actuarial balance. In fact, most provident funds include some benefits, usually of relatively minor significance in the overall scheme - such as funeral and maternity grants - the amounts of which are not directly related to an individual's contribution record. The liabilities relating to such benefits should, in fact, be assessed actuarially.

Before the Actuary can set about making any calculations, it is necessary to gather the "raw data". Since the calculations will, in effect, incorporate a projection into the future of the cash flows into and out of the scheme, the starting point must be a full set of data regarding the present status of the scheme. This means that details must de tabulated listing - at the least - the following. These data would, in general, be obtained from the current records of the scheme itself:

- the number of current contributing members of the scheme, subdivided by age and sex;

- the earnings of those contributing members;

- the contributions paid to date by the contributing members;

- the number of pensioners as at the date of valuation, subdivided by age, sex and the nature of the pension (age retirement, invalidity or survivor's);

- the amount of the current invested funds of the scheme, subdivided as cash, government bonds, real properties, stocks, shares, etc.

In order to develop the projected cash flows, year by year into the future, it will be necessary to apply a series of demographic and financial factors. Such a projection is complex, but will, for example, include estimates of the number of members (at each age) who are likely to die in each year and so give rise to claims for survivors' pensions; will include estimates of the rates at which the average earnings per member increase from year to year, and hence the proportional increase from year to year in the money amounts of both the average contributions payable per member and the average levels of pension paid to new claimants in successive years.

B. Actuarial reports

An actuarial report on a social insurance scheme will generally deal with the following topics:

- brief description of the scheme being valued; identification of changes in provisions of the scheme since the preceding valuation;

- observations on the statistical data (availability, adequacy, quality); extract from input data on insured persons and beneficiaries; comparison with previous valuation;

- description of the development of the scheme since the last actuarial valuation (numbers of insured persons and beneficiaries; amounts of contributions and benefits; investment portfolio and rates of return);

- description of the system which has been adopted for financing the scheme;

- description of demographic and economic assumptions adopted for the valuation; identification of changes from actuarial assumptions in preceding valuation;

- demographic and financial projections;

- analysis of projections; comparison with projections of previous valuations; sensitivity analysis of actuarial assumptions; actuarial balance sheet; identification of actuarial gains and losses;

- conclusions and recommendations, including for example:

  - suitability of financial system;
  - adequacy of contribution rate;
  - efficiency of benefit formulae;
  - adjustment of pensions in payment;
  - level of expenses of administration;
  - investment policy and performance.

An annex to the report should contain data on insured persons and beneficiaries, and describe the assumptions adopted - in sufficient detail to permit another actuary to test the results of the valuation.

C. Communicating valuation results and follow-up

Despite the actuary's best efforts to make it easy to understand, the valuation report will be a complex technical document. A brief executive summary will increase the accessibility of the report. However, unless the actuarial report is presented to and clarified for those at whom it is principally directed, it is very likely that the report will pass unnoticed and the recommendations will not be considered. The board and management, if they are properly informed, can use the report to draw the attention of the social partners to potential financing problems and proposed solutions, and to help develop a consensus on changes to be made.

Social security schemes are dynamic. Before implementing changes which have financial implications, an actuarial assessment of the impact of the proposed changes should be received. This is a statutory requirement of some schemes; in others, changes are implemented without any consideration of their financial impact. The actuary who has undertaken the valuation is well-placed to report on the financial effects of proposed changes.

It is important to realise that the actuary is not a clairvoyant, and is no better able to predict, for example, the exact rate of inflation in five years' time than the next person. What the actuary can do, on the basis of experience, is to compile a set of demographic and financial projection factors which:

- represent a coherent and sensible future scenario, when considered together; and

- continue the observed trends in the different factors up to date, and so represent a plausible projection of these factors from the present into the future.

Nevertheless, the actuary selects these factors - which together form the actuarial basis for the actuarial valuation - knowing that the actual figures are simply best estimates chosen from within a range (which may be more or less wide) of possible values. The fact that the actuary's estimate of the rate of inflation in five years' time will almost certainly turn out to be inexact does not necessarily mean that the overall result of the actuarial valuation will (as represented by the balance between assets and liabilties) turn to be equally inexact; if the actuarial basis is well-chosen and coherent, the many different contributions to the variation, in the financial projections, should to a large degree cancel each other out.

What is needed is to check that the overall result of the valuation is not likely to be seriously affected by such departures from reality in the assumptions made in the actuarial basis. The actuary will probably, therefore, carry out a series of sensitivity analyses, in which the different elements of the actuarial basis are replaced by values (say 10 per cent higher or lower) to check the corresponding percentage change in the overall valuation result.

This process can be somewhat simplified if we consider the financial projections in terms, not of money at "face value" (i.e. what is usually described as the nominal values of the cash flows) but of money at its purchasing power in (say) 1997 terms after allowing for inflation, i.e. the so-called real value of the future cash flows. Experience indicates strongly that the various accounting items, within a scheme, change much more steadily from year to year when expressed in real terms than if expressed in nominal terms. For this reason, actuaries would often prefer to make their projections in real terms and would understand the expected financial progress more thoroughly, but results presented in this manner are not always well-understood by a "layman". The actuary may, therefore, need to take considerable care to explain the calculation, or even rework the results for presentation in nominal terms.

Fig. 11:
"... The actuary is not a clairvoyant ..."

"... The actuary can ... compile ... projection factors ..."

UNIT 2: Data for actuarial valuations

A. Data on insured persons and beneficiaries

The starting point of an actuarial valuation is data on insured persons and beneficiaries on the valuation date. This is the same whether a social insurance or an occupational pension scheme is being valued. In an occupational scheme, the employer normally provides the actuary with the data, which the actuary validates and then applies to conduct the valuation. In social insurance schemes, particularly those in developing countries, the data collection is rarely so straightforward. Frequently, there is no system for maintaining current sex, date of birth, insurable earnings, or benefit amount data on insured persons and beneficiaries, and these data must be collected from the beginning for each valuation. This is a time-consuming and expensive exercise. Inadequate primary records, and a multitude of other reasons, often result in an incomplete data base on which to conduct the valuation. Estimates are made to substitute for data deficiencies and, given the size of the insured population and number of beneficiaries, these estimates may not materially affect the results of the valuation. Nevertheless, in general, the reliability of a valuation depends on the quality of the input data on insured persons and beneficiaries.

The following section identifies the input data and actuarial assumptions which normally appear in actuarial projection models. Generally, data which are required by age may be prepared by age groups. The active insured population and new entrants may be subdivided into groups with common characteristics. Data on numbers of insured persons and pensioners are required at the date on which the projection starts (referred to as the *valuation date*).

Statistics on the active insured population on the valuation date

The following statistics are required for the initial population (active contributors) at the valuation date:

- initial population, by age and sex;

- average annual insured earnings of initial population by age and sex (average rate of remuneration by age and sex per pay period, times the number of pay periods in a year);

- months of past service (or years of service credited under transitional provisions) of initial population, by age and sex;

- salary scale function of initial population, by age and sex. (This is an index of salaries at each age which it is assumed will apply throughout the projection period. It is used to project the actual insured earnings on which contributions will be paid).

- final average salary function of initial population, by age and sex. (This is an index based on the salary scale function which takes into account the salaries which are used to compute benefits, e.g. the period over which earnings are averaged). Sometimes it is the same as the salary scale function.

- density of contributions, by age and sex. (This is the average proportion of contributions *actually* paid in a year, compared to the maximum contributions which *could* be paid in the year, if all insured persons were working fulltime without absence form work due to unemployment or for other reasons).

- density of benefits, by age and sex. (This is the same as the density of contributions unless some periods of absence from work, for example, due to sickness, invalidity, etc., are considered as contributory periods for the purpose of calculating benefits).

Statistics on pensioners in receipt of pensions on the valuation date

The following statistics are required for the beneficiaries (pensioners) at the valuation date:

- number of retirement pensioners/amounts of pension, by age and sex;

- number of invalidity pensioners/amounts of pension, by age and sex;

- number of widow(er) pensioners/amounts of pension, by age;

- number of orphan pensioners/amounts of pensions, by age and sex;

- number of deferred pensions/amounts of pensions payable to insured persons who have separated from coverage by the scheme (e.g. emigrated) and who have acquired rights (not often encountered).

Estimates relating to new entrants

A continuous stream of new entrants is assumed in an open-fund projection. For new entrants, estimates are made based on the recent experience of the scheme. Just as for the initial population, salary scale and density factors must be estimated for new entrants and, in addition, the following factors must be estimated:

- distribution of first generation of new entrants, by age and sex;

- average starting insured earnings of first generation of new entrants, by age and sex.

B. Amount of actuarial (technical) reserve

This includes the funds that the scheme has on hand on the valuation date (if any).

C. Demographic and financial assumptions

Demographic assumptions

These factors can be drawn from the experience of the scheme, national censuses and statistical publications, experience in other comparable schemes and countries, and international studies:

- number of surviving active lives at each age and sex, according to the applicable multiple decrement table;

- mortality rates of the active insured population, by age and sex;

- rates of entry into invalidity, by age and sex;

- mortality rates of invalid lives, by age and sex. (Frequently these are estimated by adjusting the mortality rates of the underlying mortality table).

- rates of (old-age) retirement, by age and sex. (This is necessary if there is a range of possible retirement ages rather than a specific age of retirement).

- mortality rates of retired lives, by age and sex. (Usually these are the rates in the mortality table applied to the active insured population).

- rates of withdrawal from the active insured population, by age and sex. (This refers to separation for reasons other than retirement, invalidity or death, for example, due to emigration). It is not often applicable;

- proportion of the insured population which is married, by age and sex;

- average ages of wife (husband) of male (female) insured person or pensioner by age of husband (wife);

- probability of remarriage of widows(ers) by age;

- probability of survival of widows(ers) by age (taking into account rates of remarriage, if applicable);

- average number of dependent children, by age and sex, of insured persons and pensioners (dependent children are those who would be eligible for an orphan's benefit in the event of the death of an insured person or pensioner);

- average age of dependent children, by age and sex, of insured persons and pensioners;

- probability of survival of orphans, by age and sex. (Sometimes, orphan mortality is ignored).

Financial assumptions

For each year in the projection period, the assumptions noted below must be made:

- rate of increase in the active insured population;
- rate of interest which will be earned by the reserve funds;
- rate of adjustment in the general level of salaries;
- rate of revaluation of pensions in the course of payment.

D. Demographic and financial projections

Irrespective of whatever financial system is adopted, actuarial estimates are required in connection with long-term benefits. These estimates are normally based on computer-produced demographic and financial projections.

The estimates permit the responsible authorities to understand the short- and long-term financial implications of a proposed scheme, or possible amendments to an existing scheme. It is usually necessary to present a wide variety of estimates based on different alternatives, with respect to benefit formulae, benefit conditions (e.g., pension age, minimum contribution requirements), the evolution of the insured population, and so on, in order that informed decisions can be made which take into account national social protection objectives, financing constraints, and opportunities for investing reserve funds. The projections are normally prepared on an open-fund basis (i.e., assuming a continuous stream of new entrants), and calculations are then made to estimate the contribution rate(s) under the system of finance which is being applied.

Open-fund projections, which show the progression of insured persons and beneficiaries, and the amounts of insured wages (on which contributions are made) and benefits, are the most effective means of demonstrating the financial implications of a social security pension scheme. The probable evolution of the scheme can be analysed in absolute terms and, in relative terms, by means of demographic ratios (ratios of the number of various types of beneficiaries to the number of insured persons) or relative costs (ratios of the annual amount of benefits to the annual amount of insured earnings). Under partial funding financial systems the consequent reserve accumulations are illustrated. General average premiums can be calculated for various options to demonstrate, in a simplified and possibly striking manner, the relative long-term costs of each option.

Demographic projections

For long-term benefit schemes, the core of all actuarial estimates is demographic projections. Demographic projections calculate for each year of the projection period (which might be as long as 120 years):

(a) the number of insured persons, normally by age, sex and possibly further sub-groups of the insured population;

(b) the number of pensioners by age and sex and by category of pensions (normally old-age, invalidity and survivors).

Projections are an iterative process. Demographic estimates which are made for year t are calculated using transition probabilities based on values for the year t-1.

When the estimated numbers of active contributors are multiplied by projected average incomes subject to contributions, estimates can be obtained of total amounts of incomes subject to contributions. Similarly, estimated numbers of pensioners, multiplied by projected average pensions, gives estimates of pension expenditures. These values can then be used to calculate contribution rates under the chosen financial system.

Financial projections

Computer programmes for preparing financial and actuarial projections should be tailored to the long-term benefits scheme for which they are to produce estimates. These programmes range from sophisticated deterministic models to simple spread sheets.

The design of a projection system must permit realistic projections of a social security pension scheme to be made but, no matter how elegant the model may be, if reliable projections are to be produced, it is essential that:

• complete and accurate input data be available for the projection, and

• appropriate actuarial assumptions be made.

ILO Models

The standard version of the ILO Pension Model "ILOPENS" provides an example of an elaborate projection system based on actuarial principles that has been used to simulate the development of public pension schemes in several developing countries. It provides demographic and financial projections based on a set of statistics, i.e., the characteristics of the insured population at the time of the actuarial valuation, and demographic and economic assumptions, including a retirement behaviour function.

The system uses an age-cohort methodology, which means that it follows separately each group of insured persons who are of the same age, from the time they enter the scheme through the time that they are pensioners until the last person of the group has died. Therefore, the insured population is "aged" on a year-by-year basis according to the system's provisions and the application of the probabilities to survive, die, retire and become disabled. It is then possible to determine: the expected annual number of contributors and pensioners; the expected annual cash flows; the required contribution rate for the scheme to be in financial equilibrium; and the annual deficit or surplus if the present level of the contribution rate is maintained.

Figure 12 shows the basic design of ILOPENS; Figure 13 illustrates the flow chart for the demographic movements, among insured persons of the same age, during a given projection year.

ILOPENS also fits into a broader social budget model developed by the ILO. Figure 14 shows the basic structure of the ILO model family. The social budget defines the framework for overall national social expenditure. A short- to medium-term horizon is necessary to assess the magnitude of the financial obligation that the government is underwriting for the provision of the respective benefit programmes it provides to the population. Pensions are long-term benefits that require long-term projections to be undertaken, using ILOPENS.

Figure 12: ILO Pension Model (ILOPENS)

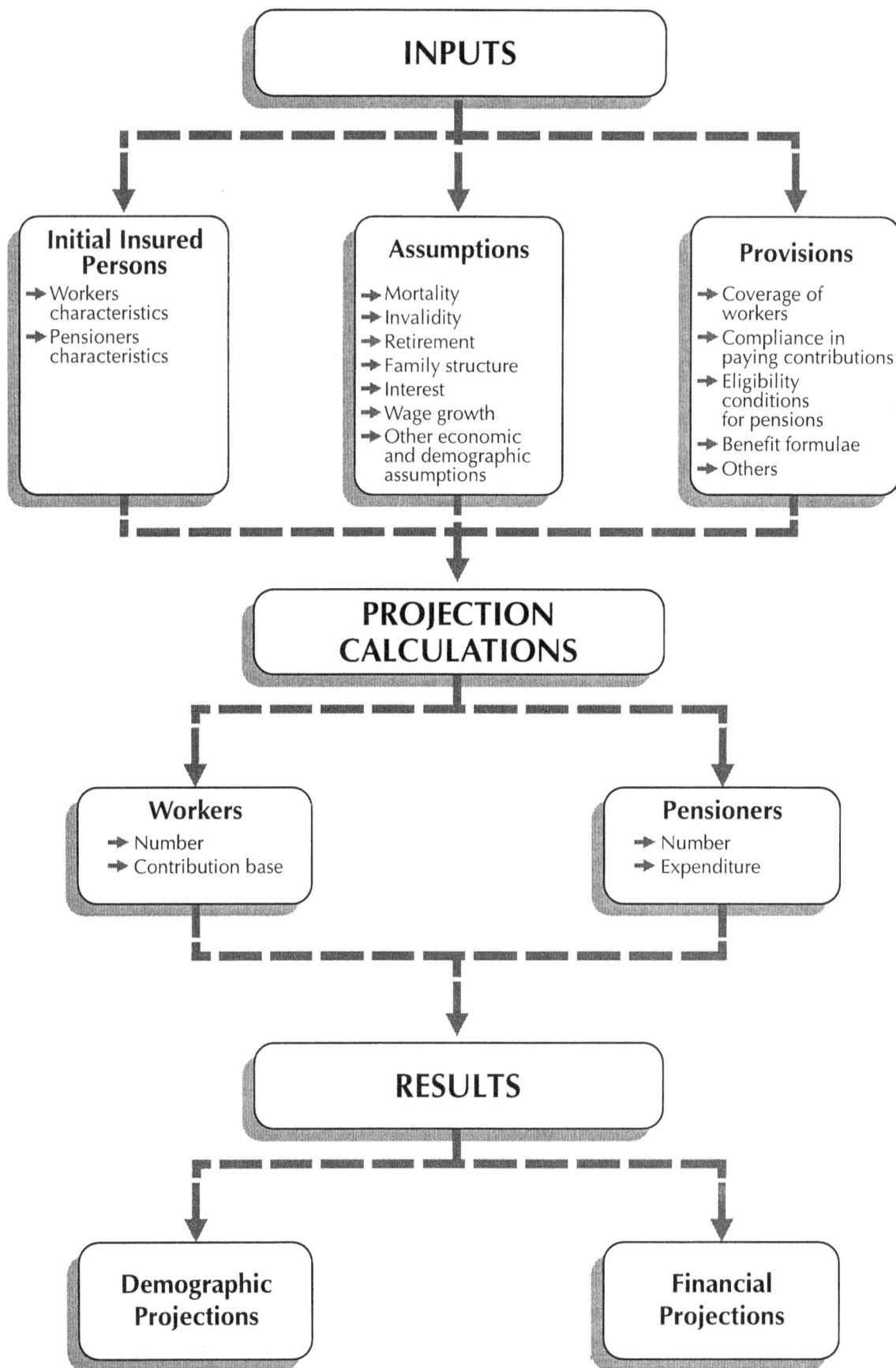

```
                        ┌──────────────────────┐
                        │        INPUTS        │
                        └──────────────────────┘
```

INPUTS

Initial Insured Persons
→ Workers characteristics
→ Pensioners characteristics

Assumptions
→ Mortality
→ Invalidity
→ Retirement
→ Family structure
→ Interest
→ Wage growth
→ Other economic and demographic assumptions

Provisions
→ Coverage of workers
→ Compliance in paying contributions
→ Eligibility conditions for pensions
→ Benefit formulae
→ Others

PROJECTION CALCULATIONS

Workers
→ Number
→ Contribution base

Pensioners
→ Number
→ Expenditure

RESULTS

Demographic Projections

Financial Projections

Figure 13: Demographic movements

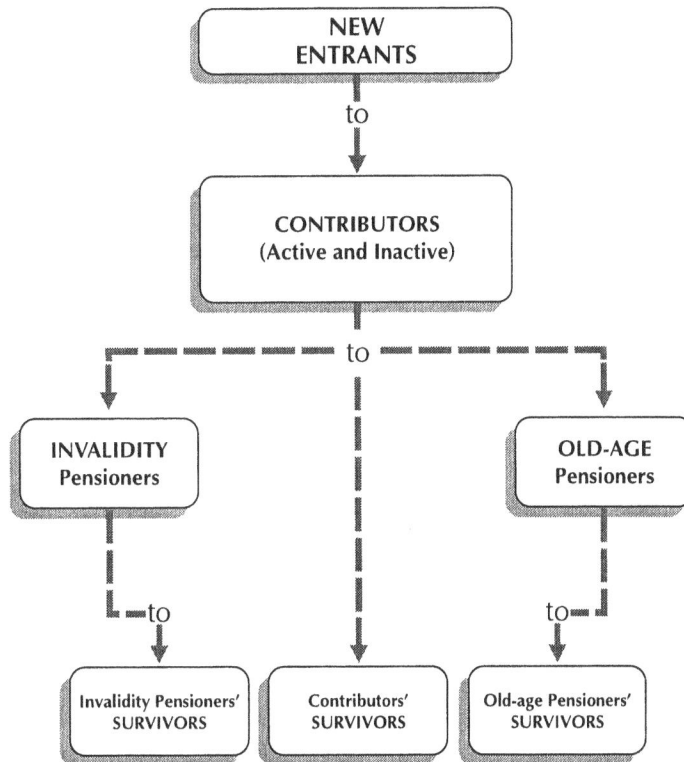

```
            ┌─────────────────┐
            │      NEW         │
            │    ENTRANTS      │
            └─────────────────┘
                     │ to
                     ▼
            ┌─────────────────┐
            │  CONTRIBUTORS    │
            │(Active and Inactive)│
            └─────────────────┘
                     │ to
      ┌──────────────┼──────────────┐
      ▼              ▼               ▼
┌───────────┐              ┌───────────┐
│ INVALIDITY│              │  OLD-AGE  │
│ Pensioners│              │ Pensioners│
└───────────┘              └───────────┘
      │ to                        │ to
      ▼          ▼                ▼
┌───────────┐ ┌───────────┐ ┌───────────┐
│Invalidity │ │Contributors'│ │Old-age    │
│Pensioners'│ │ SURVIVORS │ │Pensioners'│
│ SURVIVORS │ │           │ │ SURVIVORS │
└───────────┘ └───────────┘ └───────────┘
```

Figure 14: The ILO model family

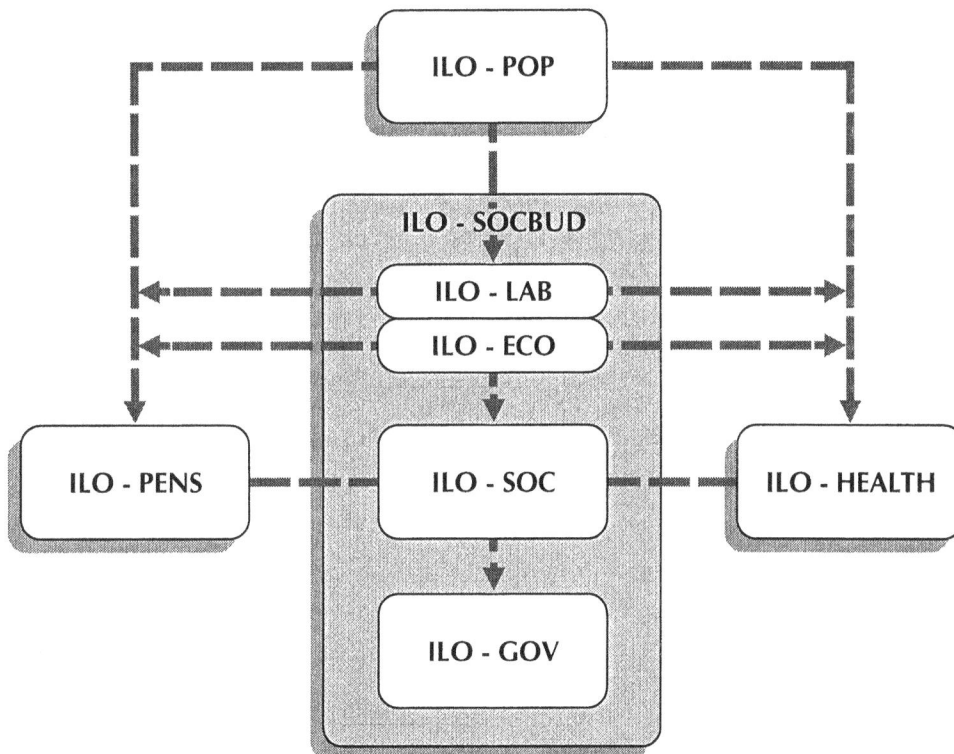

ILO-POP:	Population projections sub-model
ILO-SOCBUD:	Complete model
ILO-LAB:	Labour force projections sub-model
ILO-ECO:	Economic projections sub-model
ILO-PENS:	Pension projections (actuarial techniques) sub-model or stand-alone
ILO-SOC:	Social accounting sub-model
ILO-HEALTH:	Health projections sub-model or stand-alone
ILO-GOV:	Summarized government accounts sub-model

UNIT 3: Inflation and adjustment of benefits

A. Effect of inflation

When an actuarial valuation is made of a social insurance scheme, a number of economic factors, including the current and anticipated rates of inflation in the country, must be taken into account. A relatively high rate of inflation, however, should not be allowed to obscure the fact that social insurance schemes, especially pension schemes, are long-term undertakings, and it is the average rate of inflation over long periods which is particularly significant with regard to financing the benefits.

Inflation is generally referred to in the context of increases in the cost of living, measured by the relevant consumer price index. However, from the point of view of social security financing, it is necessary to distinguish between wage and price inflation, and the impact of inflation on the rate of return on investments.

It is generally assumed that over long periods:

- the average annual net rate of return on invested assets will be greater than

- the average annual rate of increase in wages which, in turn, will be greater than

- the average annual rate of increase in the cost of living.

These relationships have existed over extended periods in the past and are fundamental to the financial systems for long-term benefits. What is important, to the financing of social security benefits, is the *differences* between these rates rather than the individual rates themselves.

Inflation has the least effect on the PAYG system. Periodic payments, financed under this system, are simply met out of current income. Funds are not set aside in advance to earn interest, so the rate of interest is not important to the operation of the system. Inflation alone will not normally require an increase in the contribution rate, provided that the rates of increase in average insured earnings and the cost of living move approximately in parallel. However, the cost of benefits in kind (such as medical care) financed under the PAYG system may require an increase in the contribution rate if the rate of inflation in the cost of these services exceeds the rate of increase in average insured earnings. This has been the case with medical care costs in many countries.

In the case of social insurance benefits which are financed by setting aside funds in advance, inflation which produces a substantial period of disequilibrium in the three rates noted above can have a serious impact on the scheme; and the higher the level of funding, the greater is the impact of inflation. For example:

- In schemes where contributions and pensions are related to earnings, excessive rates of wage inflation will result in higher pensions being awarded. The amount of contributions will also increase but this is usually inadequate to maintain the desired level of reserves.

- Where pensions in payment are adjusted to take into account increases in the cost of living, excessive rates of increase in the cost of living will require additional funds to maintain the appropriate level of reserves.

- If the rate of wage inflation exceeds the net rate of return on investments, the rationale for funding schemes (i.e., the utilization of future investment income to enable a lower contribution rate) may no longer be valid.

The effects of these and other ramifications of inflation, on the financial systems and contribution rates of funded social insurance schemes, depend on how long a period of disequilibrium in the three rates may have lasted in the past or may persist in the future.

Provident funds

Since provident funds are fully funded individual schemes, inflation has a particularly serious impact on members' savings. There is no pooling of contributions or sharing of risks (including the risk of inflation) in a provident fund, so each member bears the inflation risk. Because a provident fund lump-sum benefit is not defined in terms of a member's wages, only the average annual net rate of return on invested assets, and the average annual rate of increase in the cost of living, are involved. The rate of interest which is relevant is the provident fund rate of interest which is applied to the balances in members' accounts. This rate is normally lower than the net rate of return on the invested assets of the fund.

An interest rate may be divided into two components:

- a real rate of return, which represents the payment that the lender receives for the use of the money, and

- a rate of return which compensates the lender for inflation.

Hence, if during one year the cost of living has increased by six per cent, an interest rate of eight per cent will represent a six per cent compensation for inflation and a real rate of return of two per cent. The real rate of return refers to the real growth in the opening balance, that is, the percentage increase in the amount of goods and services which could be purchased with the balance at the end of the year compared with the amount which could have been purchased at the beginning of the year.

In the case of a provident fund, if the rate of inflation exceeds the provident fund rate of interest, the real rate of return will be negative, and the purchasing power of members' opening balances will have decreased. Since there is no risk sharing in a provident fund, the only remedy is for the provident fund's rate of interest to be at least as high as the corresponding rate of inflation. This, is turn, implies that the net rate of return, on the invested assets of the fund, must be increased.

B. Adjustment of benefits

One aspect which can have great financial importance is the system for adjusting benefits, to reflect changes in the general level of wages or in the cost of living. The possibilities of adjustment of benefits, as well as the methods to be applied for the adjustment, depend to a large extent on the possibility to change contribution rates, and on the level of funding of the financial system.

In so far as the scope of protection is concerned, the problem is different if it concerns a scheme covering the total (or near total) population, or if the scheme covers only a restricted part of the population. The problem is also different if the scheme is financed by contributions fixed at flat rates or as percentages of wages or income. In the latter case, the contributions will follow the evolution of the general level of wages depending, of course, on whether the ceiling is sufficiently high to permit increases of contributions in the same rhythm as the wages. As far as the benefits are concerned, the mechanism for adjustment may provide only for adjustment of new pensions, or the adjustment may also apply to pensions in course of payment. If the pensions are fixed at flat rates, the problem of adjustment is practically the same for new pensions and for pensions in course of payment. On the other hand, if the pensions are determined in relation to wages, a mechanism for adjustment of new pensions is incorporated in the benefit formula. If the pension is calculated on the basis of the last wage, the adjustment of new pensions is practically complete. If the pension is based on the wages over a long period, there will be the problem of adjustment of the wages serving as a basis for the calculation of the pension. For example, if the pension is calculated on the basis of the average wage over the last ten years, and there has been a substantial increase in the cost of living or the general level of wages during that period, it is necessary to make an adjustment of the wages over the entire ten year period in order to obtain a complete adjustment of the new pension to be awarded.

From a legislative point of view, three methods of adjustment may be broadly indicated:

- ad hoc adjustment; which means that the law does not contain any provisions relating to adjustments.

- adjustment in principle; which means that the law provides for periodic review of the problem of adjustment of pensions to economic conditions, without specifying either the procedure, mechanism, or degree of adjustment.

- systematic or automatic adjustment; which means that the law prescribes the procedure, mechanism, and degree of adjustment.

The financial consequences of the adjustment depend on the financial system itself. For example, if the PAYG system is applied, and if the contributions and benefits are fixed directly in relation to wages, a complete adjustment of both new pensions and of pensions in course of payment is obtained. On the other hand if, under a scheme where both contributions and benefits are fixed in relation to wages, another financial system based on funding is applied, only a partial adjustment can be obtained and the greater the accumulated reserve fund is, the less is the possible degree of adjustment, unless the contributions are increased.

It can be demonstrated that, if the adjustment is made on the basis of an index of wages and if the rate of increase of the nominal wages exceeds the actuarial rate of interest (in other words the rate of interest on which the actuarial calculations are made) the situation might arise where the yield from the reserves in effect does not play its expected role in the financing of the scheme. In fact, the entire yield from the reserves (and possibly even a part of the contribution income) may be needed for the re-establishment of the technical reserves. It is, therefore, necessary to adopt a more flexible financial system in periods of rapid economic growth. The system of scaled premiums has been found to be particularly appropriate in this respect. As explained earlier, this system is based on an equilibrium between probable receipts and probable expenditure for a limited period of perhaps 10, 15 or even 20 years. When the contributions and interest income are no longer sufficient to cover benefit expenditure and administrative expenses, it is necessary to raise the contributions to a level corresponding to another period of equilibrium.

SOCIAL SECURITY FINANCING

MODULE 4:
INVESTMENT OF SOCIAL
SECURITY FUNDS

International Labour Office - Geneva

.

MODULE CONTENTS

UNIT 1:   **Investment policy**

    A. Analysis of the financial markets

    B. General principles for the investment of social security funds

UNIT 2:   **Instruments for investment**

    A. Financial instruments

    B. Investment income

UNIT 3:   **Current issues**

    A. Regulation/Independence

    B. Diversification

    C. Market development

    D. Management

MODULE 4

INVESTMENT OF SOCIAL SECURITY FUNDS

UNIT 1: Investment policy

A. Analysis of the financial markets

Social security reserves can have a considerable influence on the national economy. The reserves can be substantial and can easily reach more than 50 per cent of a country's gross domestic product (GDP). This may particularly be the case at the early stages of a scheme's development, that is, before the scheme has reached "maturity," which takes many years, perhaps even several generations.

Reserves of such magnitude inevitably influence national capital markets. Before the final decision on the financial system is made, an actuary should estimate the development of reserves, over a long period of time, under alternative financial systems. Social security planners will then have to analyse the structure of the national capital market with respect to:

- the investment instruments available for short-term, medium-term and long-term investments;

- the expected overall rate of return;

- the share of the expected social security revenues, and investments of total national savings and investments; and

- the likely effect of social security investments on the levels of national interest rates.

It will then have to be decided whether the capital market can absorb the additional resources for investments provided by the reserves of the system. Apart from a long-term equalising effect on contribution rates, social security reserves might be a source of investment in national infrastructure which could be financed by government bonds. However, caution should be applied when governments require the schemes to invest exclusively in government bonds and no concrete national investments are made. A social security scheme should not simply finance national debt, or be used as a de facto tax collecting mechanism. On the other hand, it should not trigger the issuing of government bonds in order to absorb social security reserves for which no other safe and profitable outlet can be found, i.e, it should not be the cause of unnecessary national debt.

Social security planners have to collaborate closely with economic, fiscal and development experts when decisions on a specific funding level are made. In any case, the determination of the funding level should be transparent, in particular to those who finance the scheme i.e. the workers and employers.

B. General principles for the investment of social security funds

Accounts showing the relevant items of income and expenditure should be kept separately for each branch of a social security scheme. Funds, which are surplus to the immediate requirements of the scheme as a whole, should be invested with due regard to the cash flow requirements of all branches taken together; the total net investment income should be allocated, among the branches, according to a formula which relates the allocation to the invested assets attributable to the branch.

The importance of social security in the national economy, and the different measures that have to be taken in the light of economic, social and political considerations, apply particularly to the investment of the social security funds. For example, the funds accumulated under a pension scheme may attain rather high levels, thus representing significant economic power. The management of these funds has to be handled very carefully and the provisions governing the investments have to be very clearly formulated, without leaving anything to arbitrary decisions. It must not be forgotten that these funds represent the property of others, that is of the insured workers and their dependants. The management of the funds, therefore, has to be handled according to certain well defined basic principles. These principles vary according to the nature and the objective of the fund in question. When dealing with the financing of short-term benefits, the contingency reserves accumulated under this branch are intended principally to absorb unforeseeable or exceptional variations in frequency or cost of the benefits and should consequently be placed in short-term investments with a high degree of liquidity. The technical reserves of a pension or employment injury scheme have an entirely different function, namely to produce interest, so the placement is generally made in long-term investments.

The basic principles which govern the investment of social security funds are the same as those of other fiduciary institutions: (1) safety, (2) yield and (3) liquidity. However, once these basic conditions have been met, another factor should also be considered, (4) social and economic utility.

Fig. 15:
"... Basic principles ... governing the investment of ... Funds ..."

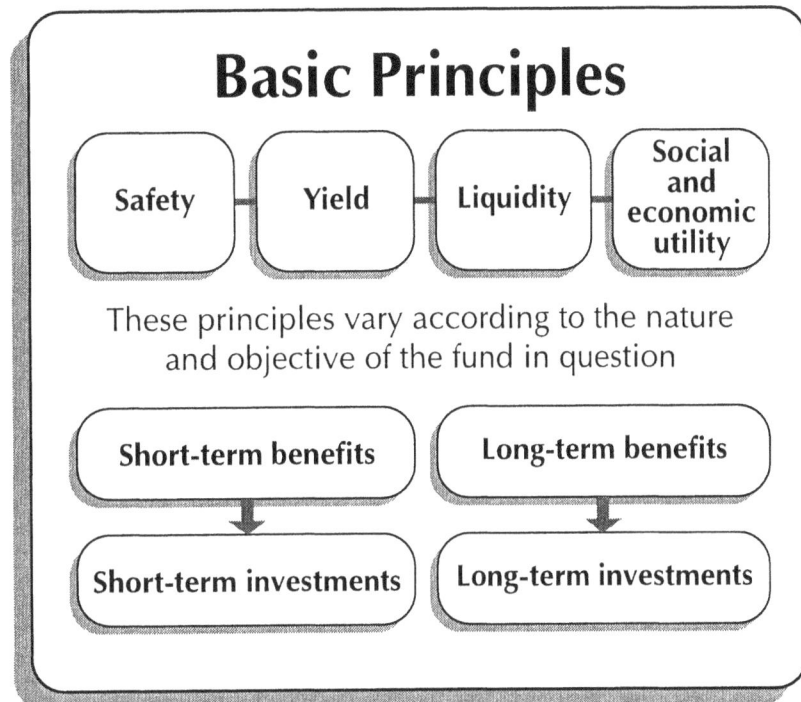

Basic Principles

Safety — Yield — Liquidity — Social and economic utility

These principles vary according to the nature and objective of the fund in question

Short-term benefits → Short-term investments

Long-term benefits → Long-term investments

Safety

Safety is the first condition to be considered with regard to investments. A social security institution has been entrusted with the management of other people's property. Consequently, very strict rules have to be observed as regards the safety and control of the investments. In the first instance, the social security body should ensure formal safety, that is, that the nominal value of the invested capital is recovered, and also that regular payment of interest is ensured. But formal safety is not sufficient if, in the meantime, the value of money has depreciated. Those in charge of investment should try, therefore, to seek real safety of the investment, in other words, to maintain the real value of the invested amounts as well as their yield, in so far as this is possible. Real safety is of particular importance for the technical reserves of pension schemes, even if the risk of devaluation is also present for the investment of the contingency reserves under short-term benefit schemes. These considerations have led some social security institutions to place the funds in investments of variable value, that is in shares and real estate. Such investments should obviously be made with great prudence and under strict control. On the other hand, as these investments are vulnerable to economic variations, only a certain proportion of the funds should be placed in this type of investment. Another argument advanced in this connection is that investment in variable values requires a comprehensive knowledge of the capital market and management of real estate. Also, very often, this type of investment involves a speculative element which should be avoided by a social security institution, whose primary function is the promotion of social welfare.

Yield

The yield of interest on investments is also essential even if, in the case of the contingency reserves for short-term benefits, the yield is not of primary importance due to the fact that the amounts are not considerable. In any case, the yield cannot have a great influence on the financial equilibrium of the scheme. Therefore, for the investment of the contingency reserve, it is not necessary to seek investments with the highest yield because the principal consideration, in the placement of these funds, is liquidity. On the other hand, in so far as the technical reserves of a pension insurance scheme are concerned, the yield *is* of fundamental importance. Actuarial calculations are based on a technical rate of interest. The investment of the technical reserve must earn interest, at least corresponding to the technical rate of interest, otherwise the scheme will face an actuarial deficit, which will have to be covered in one way or another.

Liquidity

As already mentioned, the contingency reserves of short-term benefit schemes should be placed in rather liquid investments, which are easily convertible into cash. On the other hand, the technical reserves of a pension scheme, which are primarily intended to earn interest, do not require a high degree of liquidity. In fact, in most national schemes, use of the principal of the capital is not envisaged - so the question of liquidity does not arise.

Economic and social utility

If the conditions of safety, yield and liquidity are satisfied, the economic and social utility of the investments may then be taken into account in the investment policy. It is in the interest of the social security institution that funds are invested in such a way that they contribute to the improvement of the health and education conditions, or the standard of living, of the insured persons. Investments could also be made in such a way that they contribute to the creation of new means of production and new employment possibilities, thus contributing to an increase in national income and, consequently, to an increase of the standard of living of the population. In countries with capital scarcity, it is important that the amount of savings represented by the social security funds be placed at the disposal of the national economy, with due account taken of the requirements as to safety, yield and liquidity. It may be stressed that, although social security funds may contribute to the economic development of a country, they should in no way be used as a means of obtaining money for the government to finance deficits.

In conclusion, it is indispensable that financial regulations give clear provisions for the placement and control of investments. In the elaboration of the regulations, due account should be taken of the need to ensure that investments are easy to manage and that the management of the investments does not divert too much of the social security administrator's attention from their primary responsibility: i.e. the application of the social security legislation and ensuring that benefits are paid effectively and efficiently.

UNIT 2: Instruments for investment

A. *Financial instruments*

The principal financial instruments for investment which may be available include:

Loans (fixed-income securities):

Government securities

Securities issued by statutory corporations or other bodies which are guaranteed by a government

Corporate bonds

Mortgages (loans, normally secured by real property)

Bank deposits yielding interest

Equities

Shares (ordinary and preferred)

Real estate (physical property)

Funds may also be held in cash. Since these funds cannot yield interest they are not regarded as invested assets.

A portion of a scheme's assets may be held in the form of the physical plant and equipment which is required for the scheme to operate. For example, the scheme may invest in the health service infrastructure. These investments do not normally produce investment income; however, they may be justified by the scarcity of capital to finance these facilities and by the advantages which the insured population gains from them.

The social security scheme may also be a source of funds to finance housing. The scheme may provide building loans, mortgages for the purchase of existing housing, or it may finance and develop housing projects on its own and rent the housing or provide mortgages to permit individuals to purchase it. These investments meet the fourth investment objective (social and economic utility) but they require extensive supervision and are expensive to administer.

Investments may also be made directly in commercial enterprises, that is, the scheme may own a particular enterprise. These investments can be extremely volatile and they are not easily disposed of. Ownership of a commercial enterprise would require the board and management of the social security scheme to divert attention from the scheme to the management of the enterprise. Instead of direct investments in commercial enterprises, social security schemes generally invest in development banks and in government-guaranteed loans. These bodies then provide the capital for socially and economically desirable projects, including commercial enterprises. By their indirect investments, the schemes achieve a more satisfactory balance among the investment objectives than is possible with direct investments without the board and management of the scheme being diverted from their primary responsibilities.

Government securities

Government securities are normally issued:

- to finance budget deficits

- to control money supply and interest rates

- to pay for nationalization

- to refund loans

- to finance capital spending

Government securities can have the following characteristics:

- nominal security

- marketability

- variety of terms to maturity

- low trading cost

- tax advantages

Government (and quasi-government institutions) borrowing from social security schemes, can discourage fiscal discipline. Funds may be borrowed at below-market interest rates (and the availability of social security funds may itself depress interest rates for government securities). The availability of funds at preferential rates can induce governments to consume more, to invest more, to substitute debt for taxes, or to increase public deficits, especially if funds borrowed from social security are not reported as part of the public debt. Social security savings absorbed by government are not available for alternative private investment. On the other hand, private investors who would have purchased government securities can direct their investments elsewhere.

The extent to which social security funds, borrowed by government, are used to finance capital expenditures and thereby contribute to economic growth, or whether they simply encourage government consumption, cannot be reliably ascertained, since money is fungible in the government budget. If the capital from the social security scheme is misallocated by government, the contributions to the scheme are, in effect, a hidden tax on labour.

Concentration of investments in government securities also leads to the situation where contributors to the scheme are paying interest on their own contributions through income tax. Consequently, despite the apparent suitability of government securities for the investment of social security funds, the investment can be counter productive from a macro-economic point of view. This is beyond the control of social security institutions, however, for it depends on the fiscal responsibility and economic management of the government.

It is noteworthy that government and quasi-government securities comprise significant proportions of social security schemes' investment portfolios, whether investment in government securities is mandatory or not. This reflects both the basic suitability of government securities for long-term investments of social security funds, and the absence of appropriate alternative investment mediums.

Indeed, government and government-guaranteed securities form the bulk of the investments of most social security schemes. The financial regulations frequently require that a minimum proportion (and sometimes all) the investments of the scheme be placed in government or government-guaranteed securities. These investments have the advantage of security of capital. However, due to this advantage, the rate of return is normally lower than in alternative investment instruments. Provided government securities are issued with a broad range of maturities, it is possible to meet the liquidity requirements of the various branches of the scheme. If the government utilizes the funds it borrows from the scheme for specific projects, the fourth objective (social and economic utility) can be met.

These observations, on investments in government securities, are based on the assumption that government securities *are* available in the quantities required *and* with suitable maturities for the investments of the scheme. It is also assumed that the capital which the government borrows *can* be mobilized effectively and that it is not used simply to finance recurrent expenditures. It is possible that a government might be unwilling to borrow to the extent the social security scheme is willing to invest in government securities. This can occur if the recurrent revenue of the government exceeds its recurrent expenditures and the government is able to reduce its reliance on borrowings in the capital markets to finance development projects. It is, however, more common for the government to restrict borrowings simply because it cannot utilize the borrowed capital effectively. This latter situation must be recognized when the financial system for the long-term benefits is established, since it is this branch which generates most of the funds which the social security scheme must invest and reinvest. The level of funding which is established for the long-term branch must be set with reference to the government's ability to effectively receive and utilize these funds. (In schemes which also make their investments in other financial instruments this level of funding must be set with reference to the capacity of *all* acceptable borrowers to effectively mobilize these resources.)

The scaled premium financial system is one method of recognising this situation. Because the reserve is not required to meet benefit payments, it is possible to invest these funds for long durations. This enables the government, and other potential borrowers, to better plan the utilization of the capital which they borrow. Also, the amounts of funds which the scheme will have available to invest at various times, in respect of reserves for long-term benefits, can be varied by selecting the periods of equilibrium appropriately. In general, the longer the period of equilibrium, the greater the capital available for investment.

Other fixed-income investments, such as corporate bonds and mortgages, are generally less secure than government or government-guaranteed securities and, as a consequence, are generally offered to produce higher yields. Depending on the capital market, they are usually less liquid than government securities. The economic and social utility of corporate bonds and commercial mortgages varies with the issue. The social utility of private home mortgages is very high; however, these mortgages are very difficult and expensive to administer.

Equity investments in the shares of private corporations are extremely volatile, with respect to both security and yield. Their liquidity depends on the capital market and their economic and social utility varies with the particular issue.

Investments in real estate can meet several of the investment objectives; however, these assets are normally difficult to liquidate and they also create administrative problems. It may, however, be desirable for the institution to own the premises wherein the scheme is administered. The decision on the desirability of this ownership depends on many factors, of which the two most important are: (1) the present and likely future relationship between the annual rental cost of premises and the net return on alternative investments of the capital which would be required to acquire ownership of suitable premises and (2) the size and availability of the premises which will be required in the future. The same considerations apply to the acquisition, or the rental, of other fixed assets for the use of the institution such as electronic data processing equipment.

Even if the scheme is permitted considerable latitude in the selection of its investments, the board should bear in mind that the fundamental responsibility of the scheme is to provide benefits to its members in an effective and efficient manner.

To this end, it is advisable that the investments be easy to administer and that the management of the scheme should not have to devote an undue amount of its time to managing the scheme's investment portfolio. Investments in real estate and mortgages, equity investments and ownership of commercial enterprises, may offer some potential advantages. However, constant supervision is required if these assets are to be properly managed. For this reason, particularly in a new scheme, these investments place excessive demands on the management of the scheme.

Bank deposits are suitable investments (along with cash on hand) to finance the day-to-day operations of the scheme. The amounts required for these operations can be estimated from the cash flows which the scheme has been experiencing. Funds will also be kept in bank deposits pending their investment or reinvestment in a more suitable investment instrument and, provided a suitable rate of interest is allowed by the bank, a portion of the contingency reserves may be held in bank deposits. It should be noted that excessive holdings in cash, or in low- (or non-) interest bearing bank deposits, can result in a significant loss of interest earnings to the scheme. This applies directly to provident fund members if their annual rate of return on their balances is related to the net yield on the assets of the fund.

If it is found that amounts in excess of short-term requirements must be held in bank deposits, the scheme may be able to negotiate a favourable rate of interest on these deposits with the bank, perhaps by agreeing to maintain a minimum amount on deposit or to leave the amount on deposit for a minimum period.

The contingency reserves, with respect to each of the social security branches, should be held in bank deposits or in short-term government securities. A more difficult problem is to assess the appropriate levels of the contingency reserves.

The purpose of the contingency reserves was explained in the section dealing with financial systems. No rule can be stated which will indicate the appropriate amounts of these reserves at any point in time. The appropriate amount will vary according to the contingencies against which the reserve is held and the maturity of the scheme. At the times of the periodic actuarial valuations, the actuary must indicate what contingency margin is appropriate. It is important to recognize that a contingency reserve is held for a specific purpose, and that it should not be allowed to grow indefinitely without an actuarial review of its level. Since contingency reserves are held in short-term investments which normally offer the lowest yields, any funds held in these reserves, in excess of those which are prudently required for the contingency reserve, fail to earn their maximum yield for the scheme.

B. Investment income

At the end of each financial year it is necessary to determine the yield achieved over the year on the assets of the scheme. There are a multitude of transactions during the year which alter the amount of the assets. It is, therefore, necessary to have a simple formula to measure the yield rate on these assets.

Suppose A is the total amount of the assets of the scheme at the beginning of the financial year, and B is the amount at the end. The appropriate values to be assigned to assets is a subject of considerable discussion among accountants. For example, a substantial portion of a scheme's assets are generally invested in redeemable fixed income government securities. Assets are generally valued at their cost prices or at the lesser of their cost prices and market values. Is the latter method of valuation suitable for government securities? Since it is unlikely that the scheme would be required to dispose of these assets prior to their redemption at face value, their current market prices are irrelevant. Rather, the face value or a value lying between the face value and the cost price when a security has been purchased for less than its face value (amortized value) would be a reasonable statement of its current asset value. Maintaining unrealistically low asset values for redeemable securities results in an overstatement of the rate of investment income on these securities and a capital gain at redemption which distorts the investment performance of the assets and the financial situation of the scheme.

Another aspect of asset valuation concerns the fixed assets of the scheme. These include the premises, office furniture and equipment, vehicles and medical supplies owned by the scheme. The values of fixed assets held at the beginning of the year must be reduced by the amounts by which they have depreciated during the year, or alternatively, a reserve for the amount of the depreciation may be set up.

The asset values A and B must be calculated prudently and consistently in accordance with generally accepted accounting principles. The total investment income of the fund during the year should be recorded on an accrued basis in order to properly reflect changes in asset values during the year. It includes all interest income on fixed-income assets, dividend income, rental income and net capital gains. (Net capital gains are equal to the excess of the amounts received on the sale or redemption of assets over the amounts at which these assets were valued in the previous year's accounts. The result can be negative.) Suppose this total (gross) investment income is J. If all investment expenses are deducted from the gross investment income (J), the result is the net investment income, I. These investment expenses include: salaries of the personnel solely involved with the investments; the appropriate proportions of the salaries of other personnel partially involved with investments; the overheads of the institution attributable to the investment operations; and direct investment expenditures such as, for example, bank charges, transactions, commissions and safekeeping fees.

In order to obtain a yield rate on the investments, the investment income over the financial year must be related to the value of the assets which produced this income. The asset value at the end of the year (B) includes changes in the amount of assets arising from net investment income (which has been received and reinvested) and contributions (less administrative and other expenditures incurred during the year). In order to determine the yield rate, the net investment income (I) must be deducted from the assets at the end of the year, leaving B-I. This value is then comparable to the asset value at the beginning of the year (A). The approximate value of the assets which produced the investment income is the average of these two asset values, 1/2(A + B - I). The result is the amount which it is assumed has been invested over the year. Then:

$$\text{Gross Yield Rate} \quad = \quad \frac{J}{1/2(A + B - I)} \quad = \quad \frac{2J}{A + B - I} \quad \text{and}^{(1)}$$

$$\text{Net Yield Rate} \quad = \quad \frac{2I}{A + B - I}$$

It is useful to compare the gross and net yield rates. The difference, which represents investment expenses as a percentage of assets, is a useful indicator of the efficiency of this aspect of a scheme's operations.

In provident funds, it is necessary to meet expenses on administration out of the investment income. If K is the gross investment income less investment expenses and administration expenses, then, again as before, $2K/(A + B - K)$ is the yield on the assets of the fund. This is the maximum rate of interest which could be credited to the members' accounts if all the investment income were to be distributed on the basis of the balances in these accounts at the beginning of the financial year (assuming, of course, that the assets of the fund are not less than the liabilities represented by the balances in the members' accounts).

---

(1) The denominator in these formulae may be derived in a more precise manner by introducing C, the surplus arising from the non-investment operations of the scheme during the year. This surplus (which is assumed to be invested) arises from the excess of contributions over benefit payments and administrative and other (non-investment) expenses. Assuming C arises and is invested uniformly over the year then C may be considered to be invested for one-half of the year. If i is the net yield rate and the net investment income (I) is assumed to be paid at the end of the year, then
$$Ai + Ci = I \quad \text{and} \quad B = A + C + I, \text{ hence } i = 2I/(A+B-I).$$

In the long-term social insurance (pensions) benefits, the net yield rate is significant with reference to the interest rate which the actuary has assumed in the calculation of the contribution rate under the financial system selected. If the net yield rate is less than the interest rate that has been assumed, the scheme will ultimately be unable to meet its obligations unless there is an increase in the contribution rate or a corresponding saving in another aspect of the scheme. (For example, the expenses on administration, which are met out of contribution income, may be lower than those assumed.)

This calculation of the net yield rate is based on an approximation of the assets of all branches of a social security scheme. It has been noted that some of these assets (short-term benefit reserves, reserves for the short-term employment injury benefits and contingency reserves) are invested for short terms (or held in cash) generally at low interest rates. Hence, it would be appropriate to subdivide the assets and calculate a net yield rate for each branch. Although this and other refinements are possible, they are not likely to produce a significant increase in the net yield rate applicable to the pensions branch assets if the scheme has been in operation for only a few years.

The calculation of the net yield rate is consistent with the approach whereby the operations of each social security branch are separately recorded but the investments are made on a combined basis. The allocation of the interest required for the reserves, and the additional allocations to the reserves, are done at the end of the financial year. The progress of the reserves and the size of the contingency reserves must be reviewed by the actuary during the periodic valuations of the scheme.

UNIT 3: Current issues

The growth of capital markets, and increasing recognition that the success of funded social security schemes depends on their investment performance, has focused attention on investment regulations, policies, and practices of social security institutions. Although investment failures of social security funds in a number of countries principally reflect the unstable and inflationary economic environments in the countries and their undeveloped capital markets, these failures have led to proposals for major reforms of existing social security programmes. In general, the reform proposals subordinate social protection to efforts to enhance capital formation and allocation, and promote economic growth. A balance between these objectives will have to be struck. The interrelated issues identified in this section are relevant to the current discussion of the investment of social security funds.

It is necessary to bear in mind that a funded social security scheme will be one of the most important (if not *the* most important) financial institution in a country, and statutory provisions for old-age protection are of critical importance to the well-being of the population and social stability. Investment policies of social security institutions influence the allocation and productivity of capital. Consequently, however desirable a measure may be, purely from the point of view of investment of social security funds, the reality is that the measure will also have to be acceptable from an overall, national economic and social, viewpoint.

A. Regulation/Independence

Legislation governing social security institutions' investments can be broadly categorized as follows, in all cases with or without a requirement for ministerial approval:

1) responsibility for investments is delegated to the institution;

2) investments are subject to specified minimums or maximums, in various mediums (minimums normally apply to government securities); and

3) investments may be made in accordance with trustee acts (trustee acts specify types of securities which are acceptable investments for those who have trustee responsibilities; they are common in countries with a British legal tradition).

It is not surprising that government seeks to regulate the investment of social security funds. In developing countries, governments set up old-age benefit schemes in order to provide social protection and to generate development capital. Governments normally grant tax concessions by deferring tax on contributions and exempting social security schemes' investment income. Thus, governments have an interest in all aspects of the operation of the social security schemes they have established. The national monetary authority also has a legitimate concern. Given the importance of social security investments, trading or other activity by the scheme could disrupt the national capital market, and investment policies which the scheme might adopt could vitiate the monetary policies the authority wishes to follow.

Against this background, a social security scheme seeks to place its investments in accordance with the investment objectives mentioned in the preceding section, so as to produce the greatest benefits for its members (in provident funds) and ensure the solvency of the scheme (in social insurance pension schemes). The board of the scheme (or a subcommittee of the board) is charged with taking investment decisions. Whether these decisions are implemented depends on the control structure which has been set in place by the government. If specific investment decisions (rather than overall policy) are subject to ministerial approval (and this generally means approval by the minister responsible for finance), the investment role of the board is usurped, and social security investments simply become an adjunct to other government revenues.

Members of social security governing bodies which take investment decisions have fiduciary (trusteeship) responsibilities. They are accountable to scheme members. The "prudent person" principle (USA) should apply. The board should be able, knowledgeably, to adopt an investment policy and strategy. Social security schemes are criticized for being excessively risk averse in their investments. A prudent, but more innovative, policy depends on the depth of the capital market and the investment acumen of the responsible board members.

B. Diversification

Diversification among investment mediums, as well as among different industries and geographic areas, reduces investment risks. If there were greater diversification of the investment of social security funds, potential misallocations (resulting from concentration of these investments in government and quasi-government securities) could be avoided.

The call for diversification is compelling, but the reality is that, in developing countries with nascent capital markets, opportunities for diversification are limited. There are few intermediaries and appropriate alternative investment mediums (sometimes only bank deposits). Hence, due to the saturation of domestic markets, social security institutions must undertake project finance (just like - and possibly competing with - national development banks) and there is normally a scarcity of prcjects with acceptable degrees of risk for the investment of social security funds. Rather than choosing among acceptable alternative domestic outlets for investment, social security institutions in developing countries face a "liquidity problem": they have funds to invest, but no acceptable domestic outlets. This situation is particularly difficult for defined contribution schemes where the contribution rate is fixed. Partially funded social insurance pension schemes can set the contribution rate to take into account, among other factors, the investment absorptive capacity of the domestic market.

Foreign investment

Constraints to diversification of investments in domestic markets, and market saturation, lead to pressure from social security institutions that regulations (which, in nearly all developing countries, prohibit investments abroad) be relaxed. This would enable the schemes to diversify their investments and could be advantageous to participants in the schemes.

Central banks are responsible for managing foreign exchange transactions and they have generally resisted this pressure. Obviously, they do not want to condone institutional capital flight. It is contended that domestic savings should be invested to promote national economic growth, even if the returns on social security investments are less than they would be if the schemes were allowed to invest abroad. While globalization of capital flows means that capital outflows of social security investments can be balanced by capital inflows from other sources, this principle is viewed skeptically. If a national social security scheme was unable to identify suitable domestic investment opportunities, is it likely that an overseas investor will do so?

Investing abroad exposes a social security institution to foreign exchange risks. While these risks are present, social security institutions which wish to invest abroad (due to undeveloped domestic capital markets) are often located in countries with weak currencies which are subject to devaluation. Consequently, there is a possible exchange rate profit.

C. Market development

Social security institutions can stimulate the development of domestic capital markets; implicitly, in response to the funds they have available to invest, and explicitly, through encouraging new financial instruments, outlets and intermediation. Deepening of domestic capital markets is mutually advantageous for social security institutions and national economies. However, market regulation mechanisms, (including bank supervision, disclosure requirements, and securities legislation) must be introduced and enforced; otherwise, the level of risk is likely to be unacceptable for social security investments.

When social security institutions invest in equities, questions of ownership, control, and governance of corporations in which the funds are invested, must be addressed. Social security institutions can play a role in the privatizing of public enterprises, and limits on the equity which they can hold prevent state control of the enterprises simply being shifted to control by social security institutions.

D. Management

Direct/indirect investments

Ideally, social security institutions should be able to invest their funds indirectly, thereby allowing the board and management to concentrate on efficient operation of the social security scheme. In countries with undeveloped capital markets, when indirect investments cannot absorb the funds available, social security institutions must invest directly in projects.

Direct investment involves project initiation, appraisal, approval, implementation, and continuous monitoring. A social security institution can set up an 'in-house' unit to undertake these specialized functions, or it can retain external advice (assuming external advisory capacity is available or can be developed). The alternatives have obvious implications for investment expense.

Rate of return

Social insurance pension schemes and provident funds have long-term obligations (40 to 60 years or more). Consequently, their funds can be placed for long, well-defined, periods and their investment performance should be measured over longer periods than are typical for other financial institutions. It is inappropriate to assess the investment performance of a social security scheme solely on the basis of the annual net rate of return on its invested assets.

This annual assessment has become the norm for private financial institutions, whose clients can shift their investments according to the relative performance of the institutions. This short-term perspective results in competition among private institutions to maximize their annual net rates of return. It encourages trading (with the attendant transaction costs); it leads corporations to seek favour, by declaring high dividends and retaining lesser portions of their profits for long-term development of their enterprises; it contributes to market volatility for, when a company or sector falls from favour, disinvestment is widespread since "herd behavior" tends to apply; and it can inhibit raising capital for long-term projects whose returns are deferred, even though the rate of return may be acceptable on a discounted cash flow basis.

Since social security schemes have long-term investment perspectives, they can be reliable sources of long-term capital. They can complement the intermediation provided by private financial institutions. Social security schemes are obliged to generate acceptable and competitive long-term rates of return. But they are not in competition with private financial institutions and their investment performance should not be measured using the standard applied to these institutions.

Disclosure/public information

Contributors to social security schemes are becoming more sophisticated. They are aware of the regular reports which clients of private financial institutions receive, and they expect the same information and attention from their social security schemes. Social security schemes are increasingly criticized on a number of counts, including their design, their administration, and their investment performance. When the criticism is valid, it can lead to modifications to the schemes so as to improve their performance and the social protection they provide. When the criticism is not well-founded, it is up to the schemes to respond. With regard to the investment performance of a scheme, contributors should be made aware of the investment policy, and strategy, of the board and the performance of the scheme should be explained and analysed.

Privatization

In order to overcome deficiencies of public social security schemes, it has been proposed that they be replaced by mandatory private defined contribution schemes. Contributors would select (and be allowed to change their selections) from a number of well-regulated, decentralized, competing, private schemes which would be free from government influence and investment constraints common to centralized public schemes. The investment independence, and the competition which this would engender, is expected to result in more efficient allocation of capital, improved investment returns, and greater economic growth.

The proposal requires a sufficiently developed domestic capital market, and possible diversification of investments to external markets. Economies of scale of a centralized public scheme would be lost and significant marketing costs, to acquire and to retain contributors, must be incurred. Enforcement of compliance with contribution regulations - an important feature of public scheme administration - is an unfamiliar function for private financial institutions, and is complicated when contributors can change from one scheme to another. Contributors must also have the information and the acumen to make informed choices between alternative schemes.

The proposed mandatory saving schemes are virtually the same as provident funds with gradual withdrawals of contributors' accumulated balances. It is not clear why a centralized public social insurance scheme, or provident fund, which was liberated from restrictions on its investments could not perform as efficiently as private schemes. An alternative would be for centralized public schemes to allocate funds to competing private investment intermediaries, whose performance would be assessed by the public scheme.

Mandatory private saving schemes would be carefully regulated. The expectation that these schemes, like any statutory programmes, would otherwise be independent of government interference is illusory, since in times of financial adversity governments will find a means to intervene. Interference may be more difficult in the case of multiple private institutions, and would face greater resistance, but it is by no means excluded. If fully funded defined contribution plans do not produce the anticipated benefits, and the state is called upon to supplement support for the aged population, state intervention is inevitable.

Inflation

Inflation, which erodes the real value of promised pension benefits and capital accumulations, is the enemy of any social protection scheme whether it is based on public, occupational or personal provision. Neither defined benefit nor defined contribution schemes is immune from the effects of inflation. Inflation rapidly changed partially funded defined benefit schemes in South America to pay-as-you-go schemes as their assets were decapitalized. Elsewhere, provident funds produced derisory accumulations for the same reason. Often the result was poverty for aged persons who had counted on the old-age protection promised by the public social security schemes.

In defined benefit schemes, the inflation risk is borne by the *collectivity* of contributors and beneficiaries, with the taxing ability of the government as the last resort. In defined contribution schemes, *individuals* bear the inflation risk, both while they are contributors *and* beneficiaries. In these schemes, governments are not expected to intervene if contribution accumulation expectations are not met (except in so far as a minimum benefit is guaranteed). Nevertheless, it is very possible that governments will have no choice but to intervene, if inflation threatens the viability of the defined contribution schemes and, thus, the social protection of aged persons.

Fig. 16:
"In defined benefit schemes ...risk is borne ... by ... collectivity ..."

"In defined contribution schemes ... individuals bear the risk ..."

It is necessary that contributors to defined contribution schemes recognize the long-term nature of social security schemes' operations, particularly their investment strategies. Defined contribution schemes are promoted on the basis of estimations of the accumulations which they will produce. Illustrations of defined contribution scheme accumulations depend on the continuity of a contributor's employment, the level of contributions, and rates of interest which are credited. In order to avoid attractive but unrealistic projections, a methodology and generally accepted independent standard should be developed which indicates appropriate ranges for assumptions, based on the experience of the relevant factors and future expectations.

FURTHER READING

ISSUES IN SOCIAL PROTECTION: ILO Geneva

> Discussion paper 1 - Recent developments in financing social security in Latin America
> (ISBN 92-2-110275-0)

> Discussion paper 3 - The European welfare states at the crossroads
> (ISBN 92-2-110525-3)

FINANCING OF BENEFITS INTENDED FOR THE FAMILY AND THEIR ADJUSTMENT TO THE COST OF LIVING:

> ISSA 24th General Assembly - 1992
> (ISSN 0251-1339)

FINANCING OF SOCIAL INSURANCE IN CENTRAL AND EASTERN EUROPE.

> ISSA Annual Conference - 1992
> (ISBN 1-85628-513-8)

FINANCING OF PENSIONS IN EUROPE: CHALLENGES and OPPORTUNITIES.

> P. J. Besseling & R. F. Zeeuw
> (ISBN 90-743-6452-7)

FINANCING OF RETIREMENT SCHEMES, SAVINGS and GROWTH.

> (ISSA Review - 1994)
> (ISSN 0020-871X)

SOCIAL PROTECTION IN EUROPE.

> ILO Geneva
> (ISBN 92-2-108524-4)

FINANCING OF SOCIAL SECURITY.

> ISSA Regional Meeting for Asia and the Pacific (Beijing 1995)
> (ISBN 0-644-45944-1)

www.ingramcontent.com/pod-product-compliance
Lightning Source LLC
Chambersburg PA
CBHW080841270326
41927CB00013B/3062